WAR IN EUROPE

Adolf Hitler's fanatical thirst for empire, the courageous resistance it provoked, and the titanic battles that ravaged a continent are now brought to breathtaking life in this remarkable new series by noted historian Edwin P. Hoyt. Here is the unforgettable story of World War Two in the European theater—a detailed, dramatic and astonishing military chronicle of victory and defeat in the brutal struggle between the forces of freedom and tyranny.

VOLUME TWO

THE FALL OF FRANCE

VOLUME TWO

WAR IN EUROPE

THE FALL OF FRANCE

EDWIN P. HOYT

AVON BOOKS ◆ NEW YORK

WAR IN EUROPE VOLUME TWO: THE FALL OF FRANCE is an original publication of Avon Books. This work has never before appeared in book form.

AVON BOOKS
A division of
The Hearst Corporation
1350 Avenue of the Americas
New York, New York 10019

First Avon Books Printing: December 1991

AVON TRADEMARK REG. U.S. PAT. OFF. AND IN OTHER COUNTRIES, MARCA REGISTRADA, HECHO EN U.S.A.

Printed in the U.S.A.

RA 10 9 8 7 6 5 4 3 2 1

CONTENTS

1. The Way to Dunkirk   1
2. In Dunkirk Harbor   15
3. Tragedy Called Triumph   26
4. The Fall of France   37
5. The Last Days of French Independence   48
6. Armistice   60
7. The Fate of the Fleet; the Fate of France   72
8. Operation Sea Lion   81
9. Britain Strikes Back   107
10. Britain at Bay   119
11. The German Dilemma   130
12. The War Shifts South   143
13. The Battle of the Atlantic Begins   162
14. Struggle at Sea   180
15. After the Fall   196
    Notes   205
    Bibliography   209
    Index   211

I am indebted to librarians at the Mathews, Virginia, and Gloucester, Virginia, public libraries and to anonymous librarians at the State Library in Richmond for the use of a number of books. Junzo Sawa of the English Agency in Tokyo lent me the official German naval history of the U-boat arm. L. Wayne Hudgins of Mathews helped with research materials from the Naval Weapons Station at Newport News. Benton Arnovitz of Scarborough House publishing company provided me with several books important to this work. I am also indebted to Diana Hoyt for typing and Olga G. Hoyt for her usual thorough editing and good advice, and to Jake Jones for installing my British computer in Virginia's alien clime, and to Marc Allen for keeping my computer going properly and seeing that photocopies got made.

CHAPTER 1

The Way to Dunkirk

May 1940. After the fall of Poland and Norway, the sleepy war in the West suddenly was sleepy no more. Early in May, the Germans launched their expected offensive in the West, but instead of simply sending troops into Belgium and Holland, they concentrated their power in the Ardennes area against Sedan. After the German breakthrough of the Allied lines along the Meuse River, they surrounded the Allied armies. On May 24, 1940, as the panzers were eating up the territory all around the English Channel ports and threatening to bottle up the Allied forces, Hitler suddenly ordered the offensive to grind to a halt. General Heinz Guderian's XIX Panzer Corps was driving ahead, a part of General von Kleist's panzer army.

Calais and Boulogne had fallen to the Germans, which left only the port of Dunkirk to the British and the French, and the panzers were less than a dozen miles from Dunkirk when the order came. General Guderian characterized the intervention of Hitler as "a most disastrous influence on the whole future course of the war."

Exactly what had happened? No one seemed quite sure. Hitler had been nervous about the progress of the panzer offensive from the beginning, but he was always nervous, and that did not mean he was afraid. General von Rundstedt had never liked the idea of the mechanized forces getting far ahead of the infantry. He had visions of enemy flanking movements each time this happened. Others in the general staff and *Oberkommando* Wehrmacht were equally nervous. But the best account of what really happened to cause Hitler to stop the troops on the verge of a victory that would have cost Britain its whole British Expeditionary Force was the account written by Field Marshal Wilhelm Keitel.

In Berlin at the chancellery, or at his field headquarters called *Felsennest*, not far from Aachen, Hitler met constantly with Keitel, General Jodl, Halder, Von Brauchitsch, and whoever else happened to be around. At this time, Marshal Goering was closely in touch, too. As the panzers forged their way to surround Boulogne and Calais, the generals grew continually more nervous. On May 23 at a conference at the War Office, a stream of objections to the speedy advance was heard. The generals remembered how in 1914 the boggy Flanders plains between Bruges, and around Nieuport-Dixmuiden, had been flooded. This action had stopped the German advance when it was in high gear. The generals reminded each other that the terrain southwest of Dunkirk had the same characteristics: many canals, and all of the area lying below sea level.

The panzer forces were right at the edge of the low ground. What to do? asked the generals. They knew very well what the possible consequence of the panzer drive would be: the cutoff of the last escape hatch of the British. It was virtually achieved already. But . . .

Not one of the generals was willing to take the responsibility for telling General von Kleist to go ahead with this panzer army. And Marshal Goering, ever boastful of the prowess of his Luftwaffe, assured Hitler that he alone could handle the situation. It was simple. The Luftwaffe would destroy the port facilities at Dunkirk, and then the British could not bring any ships. So they could not get out, and the victory would be achieved without endangering the panzer forces.

For if Von Kleist's army was allowed to move past the Aa Canal, it would have to take the three roads that existed. The tanks and armored cars would have to keep to the roads because of the boggy terrain. If the enemy set up roadblocks and serious defenses, the panzers would be in trouble. They might even have to retreat, which would mean an enormous loss of time at this crucial period when they had the Allies on the run.

On May 24 the generals passed the buck to Hitler. He examined the situation, he listened to Goering, and he issued the order that Guderian received on May 24: Stop the advance at the Aa Canal. It was forbidden to cross.

"Dunkirk is to be left to the Luftwaffe."

Guderian stopped his troops and told them to hold the line at the canal, and take a rest. Meanwhile Guderian considered the claims of the Luftwaffe, because he had been seeing furious Allied air activity in the past few days, with little opposition of Goering's air force.

The British had been considering the evacuation of the British Expeditionary Force from Dunkirk for ten days. If the BEF were to be successfully trapped in France, the results would be disastrous, for this was the only army Britain had. In order to man the effort in Norway, the War Office had to withdraw troops from France, and in May, there were not half a dozen battalions in Britain for any sort of military effort.

On May 14 the BBC nine-o'clock news, to which much of Europe tuned in, broadcast the solemn report of the end of Dutch resistance to the Germans, and also an Admiralty report calling for the registration of owners of pleasure boats between thirty and one hundred feet in length. Immediately the boats began to collect around the Thames estuary port of Sheerness.

On May 16 Prime Minister Churchill, who was fully committed to the war partnership with France in a way that most of the British military was not, flew to Paris with Lieutenant General John Dill, the deputy chief of the Imperial General Staff, and was shocked to see the French government virtually in panic. He then for the first time considered the withdrawal of the BEF.

Lord Gort had been thinking of little else on the other side of the channel, and although the chief of the Imperial General Staff, Sir Edmund Ironside, was sent to France to "put some backbone in Gort," he got no place. Gort was determined not to stand and fight with the French. At home in England, there was considerable misapprehension of the real situation in France. A Labour Party spokesman talked of "these bloody Allies" until General Ironside told him that the British had depended on the French army, and had created no army of their own, and therefore it was the French who should be referring to "these bloody Allies."

After the failure at Arras, the British army was headed for Dunkirk, and nothing could stop them. It was just short of a rout. Lord Gort made an odd request to London. He asked that elements of the Canadian First Division, which had been sent to England to fight, be sent to the Dunkirk area to hold the line, while the British evacuated. In other words, he was asking the Canadians to come and be captured, while he and his army escaped.

On May 23 Major General MacNaughton, commander of the Canadian First Infantry Division, was visiting Calais and Dunkirk, having been brought over for the survey in a destroyer. It did not take him long to see the situation as it was developing. His troops were already embarked on ships, ready to travel to France to reinforce the BEF. But when the general returned to Dover, he told them there that he could not send the cream of the Canadian forces into such a hopeless situation to become prisoners of war for no useful purpose.

In the Dunkirk area, all preparations were being made by the British for evacuation, without telling their French allies.

In London, General MacNaughton's decision helped

crystallize the discussion in the War Cabinet. At the top military level, it was known that the evacuation was going to come, but the public, and particularly the French and Belgians, were not told. They were still fighting, and the British were ashamed to tell them. On May 24 the British radio listening posts intercepted the German order stopping the troops at the Aa Canal and made the wrong appraisal—they thought the Germans were about to collapse. The preparations continued. On May 26 the last of eighty thousand gallons of drinking water in cans was put in dumps east of Dunkirk.

By that time the British had pulled out of Boulogne, but at Calais, Brigadier Nicholson conducted a spirited defense. The Germans asked him to surrender. He said, "The answer is no, as it is the British army's duty to fight as well as it is the German's." But on the afternoon of May 26, Brigadier Nicholson had to surrender, and that brigade was lost.

If the French leaders suspected what their British friends were up to, they did not indicate it. General Weygand, the French commander, told his forces in the North to try to form as wide a bridgehead as possible to cover Dunkirk, which he said was indispensable now as a supply point for covering the battle. By May 25 the British on the beaches were making no further pretense of taking a stand, although Churchill and the other politicians continued to put up a brave front with the French. On May 26 General Gort received an order from London to move as quickly as possible into the Dunkirk area.

On May 26 Prime Minister Churchill was in London lunching with Premier Reynaud, and then meeting in the Council of War. Reynaud asked for more troops and more airplanes. But Churchill had just been outvoted by his own War Cabinet, which had heeded the RAF plea that all aircraft must be kept for the defense of Britain, so he sidestepped and instead talked about Britain's absolute commitment to victory. Perhaps it was true, but victory when? At that time, the first British troops were starting to move out of Dunkirk for the English coast.

Lord Gort, cabling London, reported that "a great part of the BEF and its equipment will inevitably be lost even in the best of circumstances."

At 7:03 P.M. the Admiralty in London sent a message to Admiral Ramsay at Dover. "Operation Dynamo is to commence." That meant the official evacuation of the BEF from Dunkirk.

The Royal Navy was already on its way. Ramsay's staff had anticipated the London order by four hours, and ferryboats were on their way, the thirty-nine miles from Dover to Dunkirk, and Calais, where German bombers were working over the town and the French were about to surrender.

At Calais that day arrived the British ferry *Mona's Queen*, which had been brought down from Liverpool. She sailed into the port, to pick up refugees, as the German bombers were bombing. Two British destroyers were lying outside the port and firing on the Germans who were attacking towards the center of the town. The *Mona's Queen* was attacked by shore guns as she came in, salvos falling all around her and riddling the hull with shrapnel. The ship was also attacked by a Ju 52 bomber, but its five bombs dropped 150 feet away, and then the Ju 52 was shot down. Another bomber attacked them, but before he could drop his bombs, he was shot down in flames. The RAF was there that day.

The *Mona's Queen* turned at the buoy off Calais Harbor, and sailed then for Dunkirk, due east along the coast between the sandbars and the beach, in the tide rip to Dunkirk.

Marshal Goering's Luftwaffe was trying to make its promise to destroy the Dunkirk port good, but two factors were inhibiting the German air force: the weather, which was misty and overcast, and the RAF, which was out in force, with Spitfires and Hurricane fighters charging in to smash the bombers over Dunkirk.

The *Mona's Queen* came into the harbor, and took off as many men as the ship could carry, and then headed back for Dover that day.

On May 26 the British were still concealing from the French their intention of deserting the battle. General Billotte, who commanded the whole area for the Allies, was now dead, killed in an accident. General Blanchard, who succeeded him in the area commands, ordered Lord Gort to cooperate in a new attack southwards, but at the same time, Gort received orders from London to hurry toward Dunkirk. Naturally he obeyed the order from London, not that from the French.

Because Dunkirk was under fire from the German army and the Luftwaffe, several of the British passenger ships heading there turned back that day. The conventional route to Dunkirk, by way of Calais, was very dangerous, and under fire from shore guns. The port of Dunkirk was on fire. It was a difficult harbor at best, consisting of a chain of basins maintained at a navigable level by locks. But by midday on May 26 the Luftwaffe had bombed and broken the main lock gate, and so it was removed, which opened the docks to the rise and fall of the tides, which varied at this season sixteen feet from high to low. Outside the port several ships had already been sunk by the German bombers, and the tanker *Spinel*, which was on fire, was blocking the inner harbor. Only at high tide could ships come in, to the outer harbor, load up with troops, and get out.

No one seemed to expect very much success from the operation. On the night of May 26 the Admiralty told Admiral Ramsay that speed was essential because he had only about two days in which to evacuate the forty-five thousand troops the people in London expected to get out.

That afternoon of May 26, Hitler gave permission

for the German troops to resume their advance toward the Channel. But it was very late. The British had funneled into Dunkirk and set up a defense perimeter. The French had moved there in force to defend. The commander of the *Liebstandarte* Division, General Sepp Dietrich, was driving to the front when he came under fire from a group of Englishmen who were holding a house behind the German lines. The British set the general's car afire and forced him to take refuge in a drainage ditch. He and his companions crawled into a large drainpipe that ran underneath the road, and covered themselves with mud to protect against the fire from their burning car. Behind them, a truck with a radio signaled General Guderian's headquarters, and Guderian sent part of the Third Panzer Regiment of the Second Panzer Division to extricate Dietrich from his plight. So it was obvious that the going had become difficult, because after the order to hold, the high command had withdrawn most of the tanks and guns, to refit them for the coming drive into central France. So the French were holding the line at the Aa River and setting up strong defenses a little farther back at the Canal de Mardyck, on the outskirts of Dunkirk. To shore up the morale of his tired troops, who could not understand why they were being held back, General Guderian issued a new order to the XIX Panzer Corps:

Soldiers of the XIX Army Corps

For seventeen days we have been fighting in Belgium and France. We have covered a good four hundred miles since crossing the German border; we have reached the Channel coast and the Atlantic Ocean. On the way here you have thrust through the Belgian fortifications, forced a passage of the Meuse, broken the Maginot Line extension in the memorable battle of Sedan, captured the important heights at Stonne, and then without halt fought your way through

St. Quentin and Peronne to the lower Somme at Amiens and Abbeville. You have set the crown on your achievements by the capture of the channel coast and the sea fortresses of Boulogne and Calais.

I asked you to go without sleep for 48 hours. You have gone for 17 days. I compelled you to accept risks to your flanks and rear. You never faltered.

With masterly self-confidence and believing in the fulfillment of your mission, you carried out every order with devotion.

Germany is proud of her panzer divisions, and I am happy to be your commander.

We remember our fallen comrades with honor and respect, sure in the knowledge that their sacrifice was not in vain.

Now we shall arm ourselves for new deeds.

For Germany and our leader, Adolf Hitler.

Guderian.

That night of May 26 General Guderian ordered his troops to attack. The Twentieth Motorized Division and the *Liebstandarte* Division and the *Gross Deutschland* Regiment moved against Wormhoudt, and other troops moved against Brouckerque. From the heights they could see the activity in Dunkirk. But they were not there.

At darkness of May 26, the Allies held the land that extended on the sea coast from Gravelines halfway between Calais and Dunkirk at the mouth of the Aa River, to a point beyond Ostend in Belgium. This piece of coastline was about seventy kilometers long, and it formed one side of a triangle that extended inland for a hundred kilometers, to just beyond Lille. The main battle was being fought around Lille, where the French First Army was fighting hard and effectively, fending off a German army that was superior in numbers and weapons.

The main threat to the defenders and the troops assembling at Dunkirk was General von Bock's Army Group B, which had been attacking slowly and steadily through Belgium. Those troops might push into the middle of the triangle, thus cutting off the remaining British forces, which had just disengaged from the flank of the French First Army. The British were scurrying, moving to the coast near La Panne that night in blacked-out convoys. They were saved by the hard fighting of the Belgian army.

That night the *Mona's Queen* returned to Dunkirk and loaded up with fourteen hundred troops. On the morning of May 27, the Luftwaffe renewed its attack with much vigor. From early morning the bombers came over Dunkirk and struck the harbor installations again and again. They poured two thousand tons of high-explosive bombs into the town, and then they came in with incendiaries, thirty thousand one-kilogram bombs. The water mains of Dunkirk had been destroyed on the two previous days of bombing, so the town burned and there was nothing the fire department could do to stop it. A thousand civilians were killed this day by the bombing and the fires.

At dawn the *Mona's Queen* was off Calais, on her way back to Dover, when the German Luftwaffe struck again. The dive-bombers came down, and although their bombs missed, their machine guns killed twenty-three men aboard and wounded sixty. That day more and more British and French soldiers converged on Dunkirk. Many took shelter from the bombing where they could find it. One British artillery lieutenant found himself in a cellar with his men:

"By midday the cellar was becoming rather smelly, it held sixty men only with difficulty. It soon took on that musty military smell so much a part of an army.

"By four in the afternoon our nerves were becoming a little frayed. This was understandable because, as the raids repeated, they seemed to have a sort of cumulative effect on one's system; after a while the mere thought of a raid was worse than its reality."

The evacuation was now getting organized. That evening of May 27, naval Captain W. G. Tennant arrived at Dunkirk from Dover with a large staff to supervise the efforts. One of his first moves was to send a message to London telling the Admiralty to send all the ships to the beaches east of the harbor because the harbor itself was not usable. The captain sent out parties of men to take soldiers to the beaches east of the town, and one of the first groups to be organized was that artillery lieutenant's men.

But on the beaches that night there was trouble. To get out to the ships standing off the shore, the soldiers needed boats, and there were too few small boats. Also, the ships had to stand off the shore about a half mile, and the boats had to be brought in, rowed back to the ship with perhaps a dozen soldiers aboard, and the process begun all over again.

Lord Gort was now at La Panne, about fifteen kilometers up the beach from Dunkirk, and there only about twenty-five hundred men got off the shore that night.

The problem with loading from the beaches was the shallow water. The route from Calais to Dunkirk had by May 27 become too dangerous to manage, because the Germans had observation points there and directed the Luftwaffe planes to attack anything they saw. So the ships and boats had to use two routes through the sandbanks, the Ruytingen and Zuydcoote passes. But the Ruytingen pass was blocked by a minefield laid earlier by the French. And the Germans had dropped magnetic mines from the air in several areas. Knowing this, the Dover command used the new "degaussing" procedure, to kill the effects of the magnetic mines. Every available minesweeper was summoned, some of them from the North Sea, to clear the minefields. And the ships used Route Y, the Zuydcoote Channel, which doubled the thirty-nine-mile distance and made rescue that much harder.

By the end of May 27, about eight thousand men had been picked up from the French shore, and brought to England.

By this time there was no question about it: the British were fleeing as rapidly as they could. Lord Gort had instructions that his sole duty was to evacuate as many troops as possible. Nothing was said to him about defending the Dunkirk perimeter, so he let the French have the job. And the French did, under orders from General Gamelin, who told them to resist with every fiber, because every moment of resistance added to the respite needed to give the French forces in the interior time to move to the battlefields of the Somme and the Aisne.

That morning of May 27, General Fagalde, the commander of all Allied troops in the Channel area, called a conference at Cassell, thirty kilometers inland from Dunkirk. His staff then pointed out the defense perimeters. The French would defend from the naval fortress at Mardyck along the canal of the same name, then east along the Canal de le Haute-Colme to the town of Bergues. The British would defend, the French said, from Bergues to Nieuport in Belgium. In this area the dykes had been opened as the German high command had feared, and only the roads stood above the rising water. As long as the Allies held the roads, the Germans could not attack except from the air, and if they had amphibious transportation. The British defense area was only two small strips of land, and the French thought it safe enough to leave them that, not knowing that the British had orders from London to forget about fighting and run.

That day, May 27, the Belgian army collapsed. The Germans broke through the Belgian lines in three places and were on the edges of Bruges, where the Belgian army command post was situated and where the king was. Just before noon the king telephoned Lord Gort, in his capacity as commander in chief of the Belgian forces, and told Gort that his army was nearly finished and must soon surrender, but he would postpone the hour as long as possible. He postponed the surrender until 5:00 P.M., when he sent a messenger with a white flag to seek the commander of the German Fourth Army. It was arranged, an unconditional surrender, scheduled for 4:00 A.M. on May 28.

In Dover on May 27, British Admiral Ramsay and Admiral Somerville invited two French admirals to a planning session. The French admirals were surprised to learn that the British had been planning this evacuation of British forces for a week or more, but they agreed quickly to participate, in the belief that it meant evacuation of French troops from the citadel as well as British. But apparently they failed to pass this information to their superior officers, British and French, because the British at Dunkirk had the definite idea that this evacuation was only for the British. No French need apply. Armed British troops on the quays prevented French soldiers from getting on the ships.

May 27 ended then, with the British in full rout, the Belgians out of the war, the port of Dunkirk blocked, and the French continuing the desperate fight. In the air, the RAF had maintained a presence over Dunkirk all day long, and the gunners on the ground claimed to have destroyed thirty-eight German planes. German records show thirty-five planes lost that day. The RAF lost fourteen fighters. Both sides claimed victory for the day;

Goering said that Dunkirk port had been reduced to shambles, and Dunkirk town was burning. The aerial photos showed that the job had been finished, so the Luftwaffe commanders called off the attack as evening fell.

CHAPTER 2

In Dunkirk Harbor

May 27, 1940. The harbor at Dunkirk was definitely blocked, as Marshal Goering said so confidently. But beneath the pall of smoke that lay over the city on the night of May 27, 1940, the British were busy doing something about that problem.

Dunkirk was really an artificial port, built at the mouth of the little Aa River. The series of basins was dredged constantly to keep them deep enough to handle ocean-going ships, and the basins' lock gates kept the water level high enough. But now there were no lock gates, because they had been removed after the Luftwaffe's successful bombing on May 26, so the basins were hopeless. But on the seaward side of the series of basins ran a deep water channel, which was also dredged to keep it safe for ships, and the French had built a series of jetties, called moles, to protect the waterway from tide and weather. The east mole ran for a mile out to sea from the harbor entrance, and was topped by a boardwalk wide enough for four men to walk abreast. It was not a quay—the construction was of concrete pilings through which the tide moved below the boardwalk—but it did have stanchions capable of handling ships' hawsers; these had been included in the construction for ease of maintenance and repair of the mole. So a ship could moor there for a time, if uneasily, since the tide rose and fell sixteen feet at this time of year, so the deck of a ship that was flush with the boardwalk at high tide would be sixteen feet below the walkway at low tide, and the ship would be in constant danger of smashing against the pilings and the foundation of the mole. That was the bad part.

The good part was that the mole ran all the way out to the limits of Dunkirk and then to the little resort spot called Malo-le-Bains.

When Royal Navy Captain Tennant arrived at Dunkirk that evening of May 27, he surveyed the scene and decided that risky as it was, the only hope of effecting the rescue of any large number of men was by using the port. The beach operation was just too limited. Whole units of men could march along the beach at Malo, march onto the mole and along the mole to ships in the waterway. It would not be necessary to enter the town of Dunkirk, now cluttered with rubble, and a fine aiming point for the bombs of the Luftwaffe. The men could be kept on the beaches, spread out in protecting trenches, and then marched to the ships.

So Captain Tennant set up a system for bringing ships into the wrecked harbor and using it as it had never been intended to be used. He appointed Commander J. C. Clouston as piermaster, and Clouston began to assemble the army officers as they appeared and instruct them in the techniques of rescue. Automobiles were brought down to the shore, and their flashing headlights communicated with the ships at sea. That night of May 27, the first ship came in, tied up at the boardwalk, and men began to pour aboard.

On May 28 clouds began at dawn to blow along the English Channel, and as the day progressed, the cloud cover grew thicker and blacker. Most of the fields from which the Luftwaffe had been operating were closed down and the planes grounded. Early in the afternoon it began to rain and a smog hovered over Dunkirk town, composed of smoke from the still-burning houses, and oily fumes from the fuel oil tanks at the harbor, which had been set afire by the Luftwaffe on May 27. The smog drifted along the beach, east of the port, and the wind, blowing from the west, helped it spread, giving additional cover to the area.

That day the destroyers of the Dover command came into the Dunkirk Channel, one by one, and began loading the exhausted soldiers of the British Expeditionary Force. At high tide it was easy; all the men had to do was step onto the decks. But as the tide slacked, the ships dropped lower and lower, until gangways were not enough, no matter how canted, and the ships broke out their boarding nets and the men scrambled down onto the decks.

Fortunately for the men of the BEF, the German navy was preoccupied with the Norway campaign, which was just drawing to a close, and Admiral Raeder was only too happy to accept Marshal Goering's confident assessment of the Luftwaffe's ability to control the Dunkirk area. With their capture of the Dutch ports, the Germans were in position to strike the evacuation efforts with their E-boats. That morning of May 28, the liner *Aboukir*, sailing from Ostend with the last British refugees from Belgium, was sunk by a torpedo boat.

That afternoon three passenger ships arrived off Dunkirk as the tide was going out, and all three ran aground trying to cross the Zuydcoote Channel. They had to sit and wait for high water, with the constant fear of air and E-boat attack. Luckily the attacks did not come. The *Prague*, the *Manxman*, and the *Paris* all were able finally to load up and move off toward England.

On May 28 the small craft began to appear—minesweepers that had just finished sweeping the Ruytingen Channel, and vessels from the Small Vessels Pool on the Thames Estuary, such as the *Gipsy King*, a motorboat with a three-man crew which arrived at Dunkirk on May 28 to take off soldiers. The troops on the shore stayed in the dunes, where they lay in shallow trenches for safety against air attack. Officers and noncommissioned officers then herded them to the sea, and to the small boats like the *Gipsy King*, which took them out to the minesweepers. The *Gipsy King* stayed at Dunkirk for forty-eight hours, ferrying troops from shore to ship. From those beaches that day six thousand men were rescued, and from the harbor, twice as many were taken aboard ships.

Communications between French and British had completely broken down by May 28, and communications among the British were scarcely better. General Alan Brooke, who commanded the British Second Corps at the northeast corner of the Allied line, did not hear of the Belgian surrender until long after it occurred.

The confusion on the beaches and in the whole area was enormous. East Dunkirk (Oostduinkerke) was in Belgium, Dunkirk was in France. The Belgians were surrendering to the Germans, but the British in the area were still fighting to get out. The confusion continued until that evening, when the French Sixtieth Division came down to take over the lines around Nieuport.

On May 28 General Guderian's troops reached Wormhoudt and Bourbourgville. They were only ten miles from Dunkirk. Once again the troops were stopped by orders from on high. General Guderian, from his command post, could see the movement of British ships around the port.

What he could not see was the confusion and the terror on the beaches, where the exhausted soldiers were prevented from rioting when their officers drew their pistols and threatened to shoot those who stepped out of line. The men were marched into the water, where they waited for small boats to come up. Sometimes a man would leap out of the line to try to get a place on a boat—hands clutching the gunwales, threatening to swamp the small craft. The sailors would club the men's fingers with their oars, take on a load, and move off. The sailors grew to hate the soldiers; they hated the ones who had rifles because the rifles cluttered the boats. They hated the soldiers without rifles, whom they considered to be cowards. There was very little goodwill left on the beach at Dunkirk.

On the edges of the town, great quantities of supplies were backing up. The military police and the officers made the men leave virtually all their equipment. Antiaircraft guns were spiked and wrecked. The engines of vehicles were disabled. The French, who wanted these vehicles to continue to fight, were furious, but the British thought of nothing but escape and wrecking their equipment so that it would not fall to the German enemy.

The rescue work continued all that night of May 28. At midnight off Calais, the destroyer *Montrose*, laden with troops from Dunkirk, came within range of the shore-based German guns and her bows were blown off. She was taken in tow, stern first, and brought safely into Dover for repairs.

May 29. This was a day of disaster. The destroyer *Wakeful* loaded with troops that morning, and leaving her lifeboats behind to work the beaches, she raced for England across the shallows, at twenty knots. Suddenly the officer of the watch saw a pair of torpedo wakes approaching, glinting in the phosphorescence of the water. He ordered the helmsman to turn the ship sharply, and one torpedo went by, but the other struck the ship amidships, and broke her in half. Below decks, 640 British soldiers slumbered, and most of them never had a chance to move. All the troops aboard the *Wakeful* were killed but one man. The only other survivors were the ship's crewmen who had been on deck. The *Wakeful* was the victim of one of those German E-boats from the Holland shore.

The torpedoing had occurred near the Kwinte buoy that marked the northern point of the sandbank of the Flanders beaches. Here ships prepared to turn west into the deep water and head for the Goodwin Sands of the

English coast. Aware of the disaster, many vessels rallied around the Kwinte buoy to rescue survivors. The fishing boats *Nautilus* and *Comfort* came up, and the mine-sweepers *Lydd* and *Gossamer* and the destroyer *Grafton*. All of them stopped or circled slowly, searching.

The *Comfort* had just stopped to pick up Commander Fisher, the captain of the sunk destroyer *Wakeful*, when suddenly two torpedoes hit the *Grafton*, which was behind her. The blast knocked the *Comfort* halfway over, and threw Commander Fisher back into the sea. The *Comfort* ran on, circling to avoid torpedoes, and aboard the *Lydd* and the *Grafton*, the gunners thought she was the E-boat. They began firing on the *Comfort*, and the *Lydd*, going to full speed, rammed the *Comfort* amidships. The crew of the *Comfort* tried to save themselves by moving onto the *Lydd*, but they were shot down by rifle fire when the *Lydd*'s crew took them to be a boarding party of Germans. Then the *Lydd* began shooting at another vessel and it exploded. This was the E-boat, which sank immediately with all hands.

Because of the loss of three vessels, the northern Route Y was closed to further traffic, although, as was now usual, the British did not communicate this to the French. Also the southern Route Z was closed because of the damage to the *Montrose* and the danger from the German shore guns.

As the morning progressed, it turned out to be, unfortunately, a beautiful day on the Channel. The Royal Air Force was out, flying over the beaches, and engaging German aircraft that were hunting ships along the shore. That day the RAF lost nineteen aircraft, claiming to have shot down more than fifty German planes, but the Luftwaffe records show that the Germans lost only eighteen planes that day. The Germans concentrated on the small craft off the beaches, which were waiting, and vainly, most of the afternoon, for men to come out in the boats. The wind had raised a sea, two-foot waves were coursing along the beach, and those waves made it impossible for the men to board the little boats that would take them out to the larger ones on the edge of deeper water.

So preoccupied were the Germans with the craft off the beaches that the Dunkirk East Mole was ignored. There, an estimated two thousand men per hour were being loaded into ships.

Ashore, the situation was growing serious to the point of desperation. Food was very short, and water, too. Captain Tennant called by radio to England to send these supplies, since, he said, the armies were unable to provide anything. On the morning of May 29, *Mona's Queen* set sail from Dover, carrying water. She never delivered the water; she was steaming along the Channel when she struck a mine laid by the Luftwaffe and went down in a few moments.

The rescue continued. The old paddle-wheel trawler *Oriole* came over from England. Captain E. L. Davies quickly saw that the surf was running too high for him to get inshore close enough for the men to be taken on. So he ran the ship aground, and told the soldiers to wade out. They began wading, and came so fast and so desperately that they threatened to wreck his ship. So Captain Davies reversed engines and pulled the ship off the sands and out to deeper water. He took the ship up the beach, where there were fewer men, and then army officers were posted with revolvers to keep order. The ship was beached again, but once more it was rushed until some shots were fired. Then order began to make headway. That day three thousand men moved onto her decks, and were then taken off the seaward side by other vessels. When the tide rose, the *Oriole* floated, and Captain Davies loaded up once more and set sail for Dover. He unloaded about fifteen hundred troops and then went back to Dunkirk for another load of the same size.

By midafternoon of May 29 the situation had changed

on the beaches and at Dunkirk. The hysterical men of the first waves, headquarters troops and basically non-combatants, had now been safely delivered to Britain.

The seas calmed and the rescue efforts increased in spite of the attacks from the Luftwaffe. The ship captains off the beaches developed a technique for escaping the bombs. The German technique was to come in from the stern along the length of the ship and bomb. The captains would watch for Luftwaffe planes, then put on speed and steer a straight course, using every antiaircraft gun they had to keep the Luftwaffe high. The moment they saw the bombs released, they would swing hard to port or starboard, and the bombs would fall harmlessly into the sea.

But in Dunkirk Harbor the ships tied to the boardwalk could not move. There they were troubled more by gunfire than by bombers, at least during the morning and early afternoon, when the smoke and mist gathered over the city. General Guderian's men had reached Mardyk, which was less than ten miles from Dunkirk, and from there were firing their eighty-eight-millimeter guns at the port. But because the town and harbor were obscured by the smog, this was area fire, not pinpoint, and their shells were going into the center of the harbor, not along the mole.

In late afternoon the wind shifted to the north, blowing the smoke away from the port. The Luftwaffe showed up about 4:00 P.M. to find seventeen ships laid up against the mole. The bombers came in swiftly and sank the destroyer *Grenada*, a steamer, and two trawlers, and damaged two destroyers and two other steamers. The master of one of them ran out of the harbor with a load of survivors, but was hit again and the steamer caught fire. The captain ran the ship aground, and the men jumped into the surf. But at least they were safe to try again.

The destroyer *Greyhound* was crippled by shellfire and

limped back to Dover. When the Admiralty learned of
this event, they decided they were losing too many of
their modern destroyers, which had to be saved for escort
and patrol duty against submarines. So they removed the
modern destroyers from the rescue fleet that day. They
went off to begin the hunt for those E-boats based in
Holland.

The minesweeper *Gracie Fields* came up. Everyone
knew her; she was named for Britain's most popular
songstress ("There'll be blue skies over, the white cliffs
of Dover, tomorrow, when the world is free . . ."). She
was off La Panne, with 750 men aboard, waiting for
more, when the Luftwaffe moved away from the port
and along the beaches, and they bombed her. Her engine
room exploded and the engine crew was scalded to death.
The ship began taking water, but was taken in tow by
another minesweeper. But she did not survive the tow
to Dover, and sank in midchannel.

Those who came to the beaches now were fighting
men, and the difference showed. The officers no longer
had to pull their pistols and threaten to shoot men for
infractions of discipline. The soldiers behaved themselves for the most part, although their behavior toward
their French allies was not good. They continued to destroy equipment that the French wanted saved for fighting. And the French navy was now helping with the
evacuation, and French soldiers were trying to get aboard
the ships, to be denied access and sometimes thrown off
by the British. Still the French comported themselves
heroically, if perhaps too dramatically. Rear Admiral
Platon, the commander of Dunkirk, had put casks of wine
into the streets when the water mains were cut by bombs,
giving the soldiers something to drink. Unfortunately that
had been one of the causes of trouble on the beaches:
too many drunken British louts. The admiral was also
given to giving out public bulletins:

"Dunkirk is suffering cruelly, but it will hold. French communiqués have for several days been reporting our advance beyond the Siegfried Line. America is sending us massive quantities of bomber aircraft, weapons, and tanks."

Very cheering news it was, but unfortunately, there was not a word of truth in it. The admiral had been reading the French official announcements from Paris. The truth was that on the afternoon of May 29, Hitler had visited the German forces at Cambrai, about eighty miles from Dunkirk, and appointed General Guderian to command a new armored group of four panzer divisions, and infantry divisions and support troops. Guderian had moved to Signy-le-Petit, southwest of Charleville, to take over Panzer Group Guderian. They were preparing to move away from the coast, and there to turn down the rear of the Maginot Line and destroy the major forces of the French army. Once again Hitler issued an order that played into the hands of the British. Dunkirk was no longer a top priority even for the Luftwaffe. The destruction of France was more important, said Hitler.

On May 29 General Gort, who had by this time moved his headquarters to La Panne, just inside the Belgian border, across from Dunkirk, made a call on Admiral Abrial, the senior French commander in the area, whose headquarters was in a concrete bunker in Dunkirk. Gort began talking casually about the details of the evacuation, to the total surprise of the admiral, who had just established a fortified zone around Dunkirk. The shock dissipated, the two commanders retired to communicate with their governments, and received new orders. Meanwhile Prime Minister Churchill, who had never informed the French of the withdrawal, now rushed to inform Premier Renaud.

From this point on, said an embarrassed British government, the evacuation would be a joint operation, involving British and French troops in equal numbers.

British soldiers would have to play an equal part in the defense of the perimeter.

When Lord Gort and his staff learned this, they cursed. That was not their idea, and they spoke bitterly of the interfering politicians. Most of the BEF was already waiting on the beaches for ships. The men who were actually manning the perimeter were only waiting to be called to a ship. The British did not want to fight. They wanted to go home.

The French, who were defending their homeland, had an entirely different view. But not all of them. Some French were desperate to escape, and all day long on May 29 the military police and the Royal Navy shore parties kept fending them off. On one occasion the British actually fired on French soldiers trying to get to the boats. But now the French were promised at least five thousand places on May 30.

CHAPTER 3

Tragedy Called Triumph

May 30, 1940. One might say it was a comedy of errors, except that the circumstances were tragic, not comic at all.

On the night of May 29, several barges loaded with food and water arrived on the Dunkirk shore, but the supply was unevenly distributed. So, too, arrived the report at the Dover rescue command that the Dunkirk port had been so badly bombed during the day that it was unusable. Therefore, the ships did not come into the Channel and to the mole that day. Only one vessel, a ship carrying food from England in response to Captain Tennant's plea, pulled in to the harbor that morning. The Luftwaffe, believing the same, did not attack it either.

Instead, the action was off the beaches, where Admiral Ramsay sent the Dover ships. They arrived and lay offshore about three-quarters of a mile, with deep water under their keels. Small boats ferried the men from shore to ship.

There were not enough boats to do the job properly, but the boatmen worked manfully. A sort of scheme emerged. Rowing boats and rafts would get the men off the beach. Then a small fishing or pleasure craft would take sixty or seventy men out to a destroyer or one of the other ships lying in the deep water. The process would

be repeated time and again until the ship was full, and
she turned and headed for England, while the small craft
stuck there on the beach and moved to the next ship to
be filled.

The men on the shore, waiting, tried to devise methods
to speed the evacuation. A number of trucks whose engines had been smashed to make them useless to the
Germans were brought to the beach, and strung out in a
line pointing seaward; planking was put on top and a sort
of makeshift pier was stuck out into the sea, enabling
men to walk out toward the vessels. But the tides and
the wind worked the trucks loose and soon the makeshift
pier was a dreadful mess, creating more problems than
it solved.

This was the fourth day without adequate supplies of
water, and the men were suffering from thirst, as well
as hunger. In London there was concern about the con-
fusions that had built up. Just what was the real state of
the port of Dunkirk? That was the important question.
So the Admiralty sent a senior officer to get the facts.
He was Rear Admiral W. F. Wake-Walker, and he came
over to the French coast on the morning of May 30. He
spent an energetic day and by nightfall had flown his flag
in six different ships, setting some kind of record for
movement. He discovered that the east mole at Dunkirk
was quite safe, as safe as it had ever been, despite the
claims that it had been made unusable. He demanded
that destroyers be sent to the mole, and in Dover Admiral
Ramsay countermanded his orders to the ships to work
the beaches instead of the port. The modern destroyers,
which had been sent off to hunt out E-boats off the Dutch
coast, were called back.

The Luftwaffe was back that day, working off the
beaches. Captain Tennant went back to Dover that day,
having had virtually no sleep for four days. He left with
a feeling that the adventure at Dunkirk was nearly over,

predicting that the mole would be untenable in twenty-four hours more.

The problem was that there were still many thousands of men scattered along the shore, waiting. They waited along a strip of coast six miles long and at its widest part not quite three miles wide, between the Aa Canal and the shore. On the other side of the canal were the Germans, and the German infantry was coming up to consolidate the gains of the panzers. Admiral Wake-Walker saw more clearly than anyone else what must be done, and he visited Lord Gort at his headquarters in La Panne and advised that the troops be moved down from Belgium to Dunkirk and evacuated from the port.

So on May 30 BEF headquarters and two divisions of the French Three Corps moved into the British part of the perimeter. For the first time the perimeter was solidly manned.

Relations between the British and the French improved that day, as eighty-five hundred French troops were taken to England to escape the trap. There they were taken by train from Dover to more westerly ports and moved back by ship to Cherbourg or Brest, where they were formed into fighting units once again, outside the German control zone.

On May 31 the world began to learn something about the evacuation of the British Expeditionary Force from Dunkirk. The London newspapers were allowed to print the story for the first time. The French government was informed. And of course, the Germans now began to realize what the halting of the German forces at the Aa Canal had done.

The day dawned bright and sunny, and soon the Luftwaffe came, and the shelling by the German eighty-eights began again. Admiral Ramsay was growing more worried than ever about the danger to his ships, and when he heard that air raids and shelling were in progress, he stopped the sailing of ships for France. Two senior British army commanders at Dover had the impression that Ramsay wanted to call off the evacuation. They told him he must continue because of the many thousands of troops who remained on the beaches. So the ships sailed again that day.

A total of sixty-eight thousand men were moved from Dunkirk and the beaches to England May 31. More small boats worked the coast that day, and they saved twenty-three thousand men in spite of all the difficulties. Boats came from everywhere, some from the piers of the Thames at London, and they not only carried men out, but probably more important, they carried food and water into the beaches. Tugboats came, towing barges.

Several ships were torpedoed by the E-boats and by U-boats that day, but the ships kept coming. The British kept to the east mole, and the French now came in to the west mole with fishing boats and naval craft. That day at Dover a head count was made of those rescued, 150,000 British and 15,000 French. Lord Gort left the same day, with his headquarters staff. The officers left commanding were Major General H.R.L.G. Alexander and Major General Bernard Montgomery. General Alexander was instructed not to fight, but to exert all his efforts to the rescue of the British forces, although Lord Gort had previously promised to fight, and that day Prime Minister Churchill declared that the British would stand shoulder to shoulder with the French. In fact, they did not, because of the attitude of the generals, but continued to ignore the French and concentrate on their own escape. General Alexander took a trip to La Panne, which had a telephone connection with the War Office in London, and there was told to proceed with the evacuation.

At the end of May 31, about fifty thousand British soldiers remained in the perimeter, and about two hundred thousand French. Very few of the British had done or were doing any fighting. One unit that fought was a battalion of the Sherwood Foresters. A company of the Royal Warwickshire regiment held one bridge. But all along the canal, the British were falling back. The Germans decided to launch an offensive—the first real one since the Hitler order to stop at the canal. That afternoon the RAF gave close support to the troops— some said for the first time. Eighteen Blenheim bombers and several fighters stopped the German advance.

By the night of May 31, Hitler knew that Goering had failed in his boast that he could stop the British at Dunkirk and prevent the escape of the British army. Now that it was too late, and virtually the whole BEF was safe in England, Goering swung into action.

By 5:00 A.M. on the morning of June 1, the sky was clear and blue as the German bombers arrived. The RAF arrived a few minutes later and a melee began. But the RAF planes could only stay in the area for a short time because of fuel limitations, so they returned to England. And the Germans, who had no such fuel problems, then had a clear field to bomb and strafe the ships and troops.

Admiral Wake-Walker was aboard the destroyer HMS *Keith*, which took two bombs and went dead in the water. The admiral went over the side into a motor torpedo boat and headed for Dover. He reported to Admiral Ramsay on the air raid, and once more Admiral Ramsay stopped the rescue efforts. There would be no further attempt to take troops out of Dunkirk by daylight, he said.

The worst British failure at Dunkirk, and one that was almost totally covered up at the time, was the failure of the Royal Air Force to deter the Luftwaffe, and the failure was almost complete in these last hours of the retreat. The British had fourteen hundred first-line fighter planes in England, but in the daylight hours of June 1, they flew only eight fighter patrols over the Dunkirk area, each patrol consisting of about forty to fifty planes. Since the fuel limitations of the Spitfires and Hurricanes gave them only about twenty minutes each over the target area, during most of the day, Dunkirk had no air cover and the bombers came as they willed. It was worse on June 1 than any other day, because the First French Army had surrendered that dawn, thus releasing the Stuka bomber squadrons from what had been their primary task for a week. And the Stukas were very effective against small craft: a group of four French minesweepers approached the entrance to Dunkirk Harbor when it was attacked by Stukas, which sank three of the four ships.

Prime Minister Churchill gave the RAF its alibi that day. He said the British could not afford to risk aircraft, so their numbers must be superior to those of the Germans; that was why the RAF did not send more aircraft. But the RAF still claimed to have vanquished the Luftwaffe over Dunkirk; this day they said they lost thirty-one fighters, but shot down seventy-eight German planes. Luftwaffe records showed that the German air force lost only twenty-nine planes that day, ten fighters and nineteen bombers, and observers indicated that at least half the planes were shot down by antiaircraft gunners. So the RAF lost three planes for every two German planes shot down. This was natural enough; the Luftwaffe pilots were superior to the British, for they had more experience. Many of them were veterans of the Spanish Civil War.

In addition to small craft off the beaches, the Luftwaffe bombed several ships. They sank the tugboat *St. Abbs* and the destroyer *Basilisk* and damaged three other destroyers. The RAF came back at nine o'clock and the Luftwaffe's clear field was finished, but the damage was done, and again the RAF could not stay long. The Germans came back time and again that day, and in the afternoon sank the French destroyer *Foudroyant*. This day the ferry *Prague* loaded three thousand French soldiers aboard and started for Dover. She was near-missed by bombs, and seemed to be sinking. A destroyer, a minesweeper, and a corvette took off many of the troops, and the *Prague* then sailed properly again, and arrived safely in Dover.

The steamer *Scotia*, with two thousand Frenchmen aboard, was hit by a bomb and began to go down by the stern. The destroyer *Esk* came up and took off seventeen hundred men before the ship sank.

On May 31 the "unified command" at Dunkirk fell completely apart, although in London Winston Churchill was still talking about it. The problem was that General Alexander, who did not like the French, insisted that his duty was to get the British troops out, no matter what the politicians did in London.

That night the last of the British in Belgium were a company of Grenadier Guards who covered a crossing at Furnes. The Germans had never bothered to attack here, although they shelled the area. At about midnight the word came that the troops were to get out. They wrapped blankets around their boots for silence's sake, and headed for the beach. The Germans were shelling again. The destroyers were silhouettes standing out to sea, but on the beach there were no small boats to carry the men out. Some of them put aside their packs and rifles and started to swim out. Then a bomber came over, and dropped a bomb that damaged one of the destroyers, and the whole group hauled out. The swimmers swam back to the beach, and began to walk along the sand toward Dunkirk. They encountered an officer who formed them up into a column and marched them along the beach. They came to the stone jetty at Dunkirk and the *Ben-my-Chree*, a paddle steamer. Bombs were falling around her. But bombs were also falling on the boardwalk, so the men piled aboard the steamer and she began to move.

By morning virtually all of the British troops were back within the defensive lines protected by the French soldiers. The only British soldiers left in contact with the Germans were on the Canal de la Basse-Colme, from

Bergues east to the flooded fields beyond Hoymille. On the morning of June 1 they began pulling out for the beaches.

Some of the British troops behaved with great bravery, particularly the Coldstream Guards, who were along this line. The commander of one company told his troops to shoot any British soldier who retreated without orders. The commander of another company panicked and began to run with his men. Two of the Coldstream Guards raised their rifles and shot him down. His men then went back into the line.

Captain Ervine-Andrews of East Lancashire Regiment took a dozen men and a Bren gun carrier forward to a barn by the canal. They encountered Germans and shot seventeen Germans with a rifle, and more with the Bren gun. The captain then sent his wounded back to the beach in the Bren gun carrier, and he waded through the flooded fields with eight survivors. After he returned to England, he was awarded the Victoria Cross.

The withdrawal of the British here was orderly, but once again, nobody told their French allies what the British were doing, and so the Germans followed them across the canal, and attacked the French defenders on their flank. The French fought fiercely and established a new defense line while the British got away.

With the shortening of the French lines, the German artillery became more of a problem, for it moved up until it could reach the water's edge.

As darkness fell on June 1, the navy men and volunteers were feeling the tension and the exhaustion of almost a week of effort. Admiral Ramsay was feeling the tension, and had ordered that all ships be clear of the French coast by the morning of June 2 and that there would not be any more daylight sailings. The Luftwaffe had more than done its work; not only had it put a number of vessels out of commission or sunk them, but it had blasted the morale of the entire rescue effort.

And yet the Luftwaffe itself had little sense of pride in its accomplishments at Dunkirk. The German pilots referred to "the Hell of Dunkirk," largely because of the fire from small arms and from antiaircraft guns, fire the Germans were not used to and which was the most effective of the war so far.

The rescue continued in the small hours of June 2. The destroyer *Whitshed* tied up at the east mole, expecting, as in the past few hours, to see a waiting crowd of soldiers. But there was no one on the boardwalk. The captain of the destroyer went ashore and rounded up troops, a thousand men in all, and sailed for Dover. But other ships arriving afterwards found fewer troops.

Time was running out. Admiral Ramsay had ordered all ships to be clear of the harbor by 3:00 A.M., and the last ship sailed just after the hour. A thousand British troops, those men who had just disengaged from the line at Bergues, came up too late, and had to march back and take shelter in the dunes for the day.

Now head count became the problem. How many British troops were left at Dunkirk? No one knew. How many French? Admiral Abrial estimated that he had nearly fifty thousand men left on the perimeter and in the town. He estimated the British remainder as about six thousand men.

The British wanted to close down the evacuation. The French wanted to keep it open and could not see why it should be shut as long as they could hold the line. And they held. They counterattacked near Bergues and drove the Germans back.

If that seemed odd, in view of the lightning slashes of the panzers that had brought them to the Channel ports, the reason was really simple. The German line was manned now by replacement troops who had not engaged in the original drive. General Guderian and his panzers were far away preparing for the assault on the Maginot Line. On the night of June 1 the Germans withdrew the last of the eighty-eight-millimeter guns from the area, and the heavier artillery. In truth, Dunkirk was no longer on the priority list, no longer important to the German cause. Even the Luftwaffe did not attack again on the Dunkirk beaches, because the German air force had to conserve strength and reorganize its efforts against the French.

At dusk the last straggling remnants of the British Expeditionary Force to France gathered around the east mole. Some were real stragglers, drunks, and cowards who had lain hidden for several days. But most of these last were duty people, members of various headquarters units, antiaircraft gunners, radiomen, medics. Their number was somewhere between twenty-five hundred and six thousand. And also there were twenty-five thousand Frenchmen hoping to be sea-lifted out of Dunkirk to avoid capture. Nearly a dozen ships and smaller vessels showed up that evening. Soon after dark, General Alexander toured the beach area in a motorboat to find more survivors, and saying that he found none, embarked in a destroyer for England. The fact was that there were ten thousand Frenchmen waiting to be transported to England, and Prime Minister Churchill had promised that they would be taken on equal terms with the British—and they were ignored, in a massive display of more bad faith by the British. To top this, when Alexander got back to England, instead of being castigated by Anthony Eden, the Secretary of State for War, he was congratulated.

What happened next was anticlimactic and appalling. The British simply deserted the French that night, Captain Tennant announced that the evacuation was complete and departed himself in a motor torpedo boat, and then the British proceeded to block the port, to be sure that no Frenchmen could follow them out to freedom. Prime Minister Reynaud was angry, and the British betrayal played into the hands of his deputy prime minister, the ancient Marshal Pétain, who had little use for the British. Reynaud won the the argument; Churchill intervened to force Admiral Ramsay to resume the sea lift. But it was very late. The German infantry was moving on Dunkirk and had reached a point two and a half miles from the port.

On the evening of June 3, the evacuation fleet sailed again from Dover for Dunkirk with orders to bring out the French. Thirteen destroyers, twenty-five other ships from ferries to trawlers and a school of small craft, plus a fleet of sixty-three French fishing boats, were headed in to rescue the French. But it was all as a game, because when thousands of French soldiers were brought out of Dunkirk that night, and transported to England, they were then marched onto trains and transported west, and put on ships to send them back to the France that was endangered but not occupied. And there they waited, and a month and a half later, they were ordered by their government to surrender to the Germans.

On June 4, Dunkirk surrendered to the Germans.

On June 4, as well, Prime Minister Churchill summed up the overall truth of Dunkirk, even as the British were congratulating themselves on the evacuation of their fighting men.

"We must be very careful," he told the House of Commons that day, "not to assign to this deliverance the attributes of a victory. Wars are not won by evacuations."

CHAPTER 4

The Fall of France

On June 4, 1940, the day that the evacuation of Dunkirk ceased and the French forces surrendered there, American Ambassador William Bullitt invited Marshal Pétain to luncheon at the embassy. They lunched alone, and Pétain, deputy prime minister of France, unburdened himself about his antipathy to the British.

As long as the British Expeditionary Force had been in France, he said, the British Royal Air Force had fought valiantly and effectively. But when the Germans had broken through and cut off the Allied armies from the forces on the Maginot Line, the British had insisted that their army be evacuated at Dunkirk, and had let the French do all the fighting to preserve the enclave for the British escape.

Further, at the moment that the French were fighting a battle for survival, said Pétain, the British had pretended that they had no reserves in England, and they had refused to send more aircraft to fight the battle.

In fact, Marshal Pétain was wrong about the British reserves, although he was quite right about the air force. The British had been very careless and inept during the peace years and had allowed their armed forces to deteriorate to the point of disaster. It was true that they had no reserves. The few troops who could have been committed had been sent to Norway, and even these had been augmented by pulling a division out of France and putting that, too, in Norway. There were men in Britain who would be soldiers, but they were not soldiers yet.

But Churchill was doing the best he could do. The Fifty-second British Division was ready to sail and ordered to move on June 7. The Third Division, under General Montgomery, was being reequipped in England, and prepared to go back into France. The First Canadian Division, held back from sailing to Dunkirk, was now prepared to arrive in Brest on June 11.

As for the air force, here it was a question of the professionals, the air marshals, challenging Prime Minister Churchill and winning the battle in the War Cabinet. Churchill had wanted to commit the Royal Air Force fully to the French battles, but the RAF leaders had balked, and by artful lobbying, they had defeated Churchill in the cabinet vote on the subject. There was no greater advocate of British-French unity than Churchill, but unfortunately, his view was not shared in the armed services, whose arrogance and provinciality were unparalleled. Even Anthony Eden, the Secretary of State for War, would listen to Churchill's demands to help the French and to bear the British share of the burden at Dunkirk, and then Eden would quietly encourage Lord Gort in his insistence that the only important matter was to save the British Expeditionary Force, and not to fight the Germans.

Pétain believed the British intended to shed the last drop of French blood in their narrow British interest. After the French had bled to death, he said, he was sure the British would make a quick peace with Hitler, which might even involve the British government turning fascist.

Under the circumstances, said the marshal, unless the British acted immediately to send troops and planes, then the French should come immediately to terms with Germany, and let England play its own hand.

Ambassador Bullitt, who was no lover of Britain

either, was very much impressed with Marshal Pétain's arguments, and the next day, June 5, he called on Premier Reynaud. Reynaud agreed with much that Pétain had said, and told Bullitt that he had that very morning sent a very stiff note to Churchill in London. Ambassador Bullitt communicated with President Roosevelt and Secretary of State Cordell Hull, suggesting that the British were saving their air force as a negotiating point with the Germans, but the president and the Secretary of State continued to have faith in Churchill's determination to fight on, and were equally certain that the French were finished. Too dispirited to fight, was the conclusion.

Churchill, too, had concluded that the French were finished, and on June 5 he communicated his doubts to Mackenzie King, the prime minister of Canada. "I do not know whether it will be possible to keep France in the war or not. I hope they will, even at the worst, maintain a gigantic guerilla [sic]."

General von Rundstedt on that June 5 sat just outside Dunkirk, and watched the British escaping by the thousands, and fretted. As he recalled:

"I was kept uselessly outside the port, unable to move. I recommended to the Supreme Command that my five panzer divisions be immediately sent into the town and thereby completely destroy the retreating English. But I received definite orders from the führer that under no circumstances was I to attack, and I was expressly forbidden to send any of my troops closer than ten kilometers from Dunkirk. The only weapons I was permitted to use against the English were my medium guns. At this distance I sat outside the town, watching the English escape, while my tanks and infantry were prohibited from moving."

Rundstedt blamed Hitler for what he called "this incredible blunder." Hitler, he said, received daily reports of tank losses, and by using arithmetic, he deduced that his army did not have enough armor to attack the British.

What he did not seem to realize was that a tank reported out of order one day might be in action the next day. The second reason for Hitler's caution was that from the maps in his office, he gathered that all the land around Dunkirk was flooded. So he held Von Rundstedt in check for the southern drive against the remnants of the Allied forces. At 9:00 A.M. on June 4, the French First Army surrendered, after having fought bravely to assure the salvation of 200,000 members of the BEF and 120,000 Frenchmen. The Allies had lost sixty-one divisions, half the total with which they had begun the battle three weeks earlier. The French had lost their best units, almost all the armor and motorized troops, and half the modern artillery. And the day after the fall of Dunkirk, the German offensive was renewed. The French had only sixty divisions left; the Germans had twice as many, and nearly ten times as much armor. The British had only one British infantry division left in France, and part of an armored division. Since the RAF had withdrawn from French bases, the Luftwaffe had undisputed control of the air.

On June 5 Premier Reynaud appointed Charles de Gaulle, commander of the Fourth Armored Division, as under secretary of the Ministry of National Defense. General Weygand, who did not like De Gaulle, was most unhappy. "He's an infant," Weygand protested. Marshal Pétain thought even less of De Gaulle than Weygand. The old vice premier thought De Gaulle an ungrateful and arrogant man. He lamented the appointment. But the fact was that De Gaulle was a fighting man, and Weygand and Pétain were both already beaten.

Southwest of Charleville, General Guderian assembled his new Panzer Group Guderian, which consisted of the XXXIX Army Corps, with the First and Second Panzer divisions and the Twenty-ninth Motorized Infantry Division, and the XLI Army Corps, with the Sixth and Eighth Panzer divisions and the Twentieth Motorized Infantry. There the troops waited for the signal to resume the offensive against the French. The Germans had already destroyed the bulk of the French armored strength, so the second phase of the campaign should be considerably easier. The remainder of the French army consisted of seventy divisions, and two British divisions were still in France, having been cut off from the beaches by the German attack.

The Army Group Von Bock was ready to start action by June 5. At dawn they attacked. General Weygand issued his order of the day:

"The battle of France has begun . . . The fate of our country, the safeguarding of her liberties, the future of our children, depends on your tenacity."

Did Weygand really believe it? Certainly Marshal Pétain did not. He was so imbued with detestation of the British that he seemed to welcome a rapprochemont with the Germans, and that is what he expected. As for Weygand, he seemed more concerned with the glory of his defeat than anything else. His new obsession was to maintain law and order. He forbade retreat to Africa or to England. It was to be "a battle without hope," as the French war historians would call it.

The forty-three divisions the French had been able to bring forward to oppose the Germans included three armored divisions and three cavalry. But they had a two-hundred mile front to defend, on the other side of which were massed the ninety-five German divisions, ten of them panzers. The Germans also brought up two air fleets.

In the center of the line, the Kleist Group ran into heavy resistance from the French Seventh Army on the Somme River between Amiens and Ceronne. After two days of fighting, the French still held.

But on the flanks the situation was different. On June 7 General Rommel's Seventh Panzer Division, which had led the Fifteenth Panzer Corps to a point ten miles south of the Somme, broke through the French line and advanced another ten miles to Forges-les-Eaux, only twenty-four miles from Rouen, on the Seine River. This thrust cut the French Tenth Army in two, leaving two French infantry divisions, two French cavalry divisions, and one British division isolated, their backs to the sea.

On June 8, the Germans reached the lower Seine and a point only forty miles from Paris. In four days the panzers had cleared the way for the assault on Paris.

General von Rundstedt's Army Group A, which had been held back in the Dunkirk area, would not be ready until June 9. The Von Rundstedt Group was to cross the Aisne River and the Aisne Canal between Château-Porcien and Attigny and then push south. They would break through the Weygand Line, cross at eight different points, and after establishing the bridgehead, General Guderian's Panzer units were to attack through the infantry, and then advance rapidly toward Paris or Langres or Verdun.

The German high command shifted four panzer divisions from the Somme to Von Rundstedt on the Aisne. If the attack worked properly, it would pinch Paris from the east and from the Maginot Line.

As usual, General Guderian was impatient with delay. He wanted certain crossing places left for the panzer divisions, but the Twelfth Army command refused his request, and so the panzers lined up behind the infantry and waited for them to cross and seize the bridgeheads.

The attack began on June 9. Again the French fought valiantly, and by noon the infantry had managed to seize only one bridgehead at Château-Porcien. Guderian then asked Twelfth Army to let his tanks assemble in that bridgehead that night so they could attack the next morning. So they were stalled.

On June 10 Premier Reynaud held a meeting with his generals. General de Gaulle suggested that the armies retreat to Brittany and hold out there as long as possible. He had no hopes of winning, but if the armies moved into Brittany, the stage would be set for a move to North Africa and a continuation of the battle against the Germans there. Algeria and Morocco would be the keys to French survival. But General Weygand had already made up his mind to seek accommodation with the Germans. He would not hear of it.

At 4:00 P.M. on June 10 the French ambassador to Italy telephoned to announce that Mussolini, who had so far refused to enter the war and fight, had decided now that the war was nearly over and he would "help" Hitler and share in the spoils. He would declare war on France and Britain at midnight.

De Gaulle looked around him that evening. "The evidence of the collapse was there for all to see. The government was leaving Paris that evening. The withdrawal of the front accelerated. Italy declared war. But at the summit of the state, the tragedy played itself out as in a dream. At certain moments, even, you could have believed that a sort of terrible humor spiced the fall of France, rolling from the heights of history down to the lowest depths of the abyss."

The government left Paris that night, moving south to the Loire country, to Orleans, for the civil government, and nearby Briare for the new military general headquarters. Most of the officials went by automobile, and it was rough going, because eight million French refugees crowded the roads, trying desperately to escape the advancing Germans.

The local Paris military commander was prepared to defend the city to the last, but General Weygand had other ideas. On the night of June 10 he said:

"Paris is an Open City. In order that Paris shall preserve its character as an Open City, it is my intention to avoid any defensive organization around the city on the old belt of the old fortifications or on that of the ancient forts."

But it was two days before anyone knew of the Weygand decision. The newspapers had quit publication on the night the government fled.

On June 10 the German attacks met virtually no resistance. In the afternoon the Germans captured Juniville after a tank battle. The Germans won, but they suffered heavy casualties.

On June 11 Premier Reynaud cabled Churchill asking that the Supreme Allied War Council meet at the new headquarters at Briare, and Churchill flew to France, taking Anthony Eden and General Dill and General Ismay. The prime minister's plane had an escort of twelve Hurricane fighters. They landed and Churchill was immediately impressed by the unresponsiveness of the French. They went to the chateau where they would meet and found Prime Minister Reynaud, Marshal Pétain, General Weygand, and several others, including De Gaulle. At seven o'clock at night they began a conference.

Churchill urged the French to defend Paris. Pétain said it was foolish. Weygand said they were approaching the decisive moment and called for British air support on a massive scale. But Churchill, knowing that his cabinet would not agree, replied:

"This is not the decisive point and this is not the decisive moment. That moment will come when Hitler hurls his Luftwaffe against Great Britain. If we can keep command of the air, and if we can keep the seas open, as we certainly shall keep them open, we will win it all back for you."

No, he said. No aircraft. Twenty-five fighter squadrons had to be maintained for the defense of Britain, and nothing would make the British give them up.

Churchill then pleaded with the French to begin guerrilla activity if, as they said, their armies were finished. He said the French, continuing to fight, could hold down a hundred German divisions. Weygand replied that "even if that were so, they would still have another hundred to invade and conquer you. What would you do then?''

Effectively that was the end of the discussion. They talked on for a while, and then they dined. Churchill had made arrangements for the movement of a force of heavy British bombers to airfields near Marseilles, expecting the Italians to enter the war. When they entered, the British would strike hard with a bombing raid. But this night, when the event had occurred, Air Vice Marshal Barratt, commander of the British air forces in France, reported that the attack had failed. The French authorities had first objected to the British using French fields to bomb Italy, and then Reynaud had countermanded those orders. But French people near the airfields had dragged carts and wagons onto the fields and made it impossible for the bombers to take off.

After dinner, over coffee and brandy, Reynaud informed Churchill that Pétain wanted France to seek an armistice with the Germans.

They adjourned and went to bed but agreed to meet again on the morning of June 12. At the morning meeting, Premier Reynaud renewed his plea for five squadrons of British fighter planes, and Weygand asked for bombers. Churchill said he would take it up with the War Cabinet when he went back to London, but he already knew the answer. It would be no. The meeting soon ended, because it was obvious that the British and French were talking at each other and not to each other. Churchill did his best to persuade the French to stay in the war, somehow, but it was obvious that Weygand and Pétain's minds were set on surrender. They no longer trusted their British allies; it was quite apparent in the meetings. Churchill ended with a plea that France stay in the struggle ''to prolong the resistance until the United States comes in.'' And then the meeting adjourned and that was the last the British saw of the French. The Supreme War Council was a thing of the past.

The German XXXIX Army Corps moved against Châlons-sur-Marne. The French counterattacked vigorously, but the Germans were too much for them. On June 12 Reims was in German hands. On June 11 the British and French troops near the mouth of the Seine had been cornered at a small fishing port between Dieppe and Le Havre, by the Fifth and Seventh German Panzer divisions. That night the Royal Navy sent destroyers to evacuate the men, but they could not come into the port because of heavy fog. Next morning, June 12, as Churchill's party flew back to London, forty thousand men surrendered, including eight thousand British soldiers.

On June 13 the First Panzer Division reached the Rhine-Marne Canal and put a bridgehead over it, but again, higher authority made them stop. Guderian bent his orders again, and gave permission for the troops to move ahead. On the night of June 13, the forward German elements began to enter the suburbs of Paris, and the French accepted the terms offered by the Germans:

There would be no resistance in the Paris area. There would be no destruction of bridges or public services, in particular the water system, and electricity, and communications. The police would maintain law and order, and for the first forty-eight hours of the occupation, the population would remain indoors. On the morning of June 14, troops of the German Ninth Division began to march into Paris without opposition. General Bock, commander of Army Group B, hurried into Paris and held a review of the troops of the Ninth Division at the Place de la Concorde, and then watched the troops of the Eighth and Twenty-eighth divisions as they marched through the Arc de Triomphe. Then he drove to the Invalides to take a look at the tomb of Napoleon. That day the swastika flag of Nazi Germany was hoisted atop the Eiffel Tower.

The French government fled again, from its temporary stopping place in the Loire valley to Bordeaux in south-western France. It was apparent in London and Washington that the end was very near.

CHAPTER 5

The Last Days of French Independence

On June 11 the government of France, in complete disarray after the flight from Paris, tried to reestablish itself in the old Loire castles and chateaux. The ministries were perhaps thirty miles apart, and the combination—lack of telephones and crowds of refugees on the highways—made it almost impossible for the ministries to communicate with one another. The French Foreign Office got its news from abroad by using the British ambassador's portable radio.

Before the arrival of Winston Churchill, General Weygand wrote an order for a general retreat, abandoning the Maginot Line and moving back from a line starting with Caen at the bottom of the Cherbourg Peninsula, to the south of the Loire, and then east to the Swiss border. Temporarily he held on to the order.

When Churchill returned to England, he told the War Cabinet that all was lost, France was going to get out of the war, and that the British must now concentrate their efforts on the defense of their island. When Churchill was gone, on the afternoon on June 12, General Weygand issued his order of general retreat. Later that afternoon, Weygand drove over the crowded road to the chateau where the president of the republic was installed. A cabinet meeting was scheduled for 7:00 A.M., and although

Weygand, as a soldier, had no right to be there, he joined the twenty-three ministers who had also come. The general had something to say: France was defeated. He demanded that the government ask the Germans for an armistice.

The demand stunned the cabinet ministers. Premier Reynaud tried to rally them, proposing that the government move to Brittany immediately and then to North Africa if necessary. Nothing was decided that day; Churchill was invited back for the final meeting of the Allied Supreme Council on June 13. After that ended and Churchill returned for the last time to London, Marshal Pétain began a conspiracy to unseat Premier Reynaud. On June 14, what Reynaud regarded as France's last hope was dashed when President Roosevelt, who had been asked to declare war on Germany, told the French that action was not within his constitutional powers.

Reynaud set out that morning of June 14 for Bordeaux, and U.S. chargé d'affaires Anthony J. Drexel Biddle noted that Reynaud was extremely depressed and that if the United States did not take some positive action very soon, the French government would surrender to the Germans.

By the time Reynaud arrived at Bordeaux, the city was seething with conspiracies aiming at his downfall. Principal among the conspirators was Pierre Laval, a right-wing politician whose dream was the destruction of the Third Republic and the establishment of a fascist government akin to Nazi Germany and Fascist Italy. He proposed to ally himself with Marshal Pétain.

On June 15 Weygand and Reynaud argued about the future. Weygand wanted to surrender; Reynaud agreed that the military situation was disastrous, but he wanted a cease-fire with no surrender. At the cabinet meeting that followed, Reynaud tried to rally his ministers around him and failed. He tried one last time to persuade America to help, telling President Roosevelt in a cable that

France had only two choices, to surrender or to move to North Africa and fight. Roosevelt simply reiterated his statement that he had no right to take action, that that was the prerogative of the American Congress.

And so on June 16 the struggle continued within the cabinet. Vice Premier Pétain announced that day that he would resign, because he could no longer remain in a government that refused to bring an end to the war that was destroying France. The ploy failed when Reynaud refused to accept the resignation. Then a bit later came word from Churchill in London. The British prime minister had previously insisted that France was committed to fight on and had no right to make a separate peace. Reynaud had asked for permission to make peace, and now Churchill replied that only if the French fleet was sailed over to England would he countenance the action.

Later in the day, through General de Gaulle, who was in London, Churchill and Reynaud agreed on a declaration of union between France and Britain. This would be real union; French citizens would also be British citizens, and vice versa. Reynaud went into the cabinet meeting at 5:00 P.M. on June 16 feeling that he had won, that the declaration of union would persuade the ministers to back him to the hilt. But to the contrary, the ministers greeted his proposal with stony silence, and some of them said they would reject such an idea outright. Such was the distrust of the British in France that Dunkirk had engendered.

One politician said the British were trying to reduce France to the status of a dominion. Another said that Britain would soon be overrun by the Germans, so such a union would be like marriage to a cadaver. The cabinet having turned against Reynaud, that day he met with President Le Brun, who asked him to arrange an armistice with the Germans. Reynaud said he could not do it, and suggested that Le Brun appoint Marshal Pétain to the prime ministry, and Pétain would make the armistice.

So the eighty-four-year-old marshal became prime minister of France. General de Gaulle, learning that the marshal's minister of defense would be General Weygand, decided to flee to London before he could be arrested, as he believed he would be since Weygand disliked him so much, and De Gaulle had held out constantly for continuing the fight against the Germans. A British plane had come to the field at Bordeaux to pick up General Edward Spears, the British representative of Prime Minister Churchill, and De Gaulle pretended to be seeing Spears off, and then boarded the plane at the last moment. He arrived in London, called on Prime Minister Churchill, and then settled down to become "the conscience of France."

Back in Bordeaux, Marshal Pétain took the reins of government that same night of June 16, and in half an hour the decision was made that the government would seek an armistice with Germany. The 107th and last government of the Third Republic had just decided to commit suicide.

The German armies advanced swiftly through France. General Guderian's panzers moved east of the Marne, and Von Kleist's group advanced towards Dijon. Group headquarters kept moving up, heading toward the Swiss border. On June 16, the day the Reynaud government collapsed, the First Panzer Division captured a bridge over the Saône River. On June 17 Guderian's Twenty-ninth Motorized Division reached the Swiss frontier, so quickly that Hitler did not believe Guderian's report, and General Guderian had to assure him that Guderian was actually on the Swiss border himself. Soon Guderian linked up with the German Seventh Army and cut off French army communications from Alsace-Lorraine with the rest of France. On June 18 Guderian was in Belfort. The First Panzer Division moved north of Belfort, capturing prisoners now by the thousands. The French in Alsace-Lorraine were almost entirely surrounded.

In short order the Germans captured three important fortresses, each rendering about forty thousand prisoners of war. Contact with the Seventh Army was made on June 19, at La Chapelle northeast of Belfort. The Wehrmacht also captured several forts along the Moselle valley, and through the Vosges mountains. The prisoners were coming in so rapidly that the German generals had difficulty counting, and Colonel General Ritter von Leeb was chosen to adjudicate claims of valor. He gave Guderian credit for 150,000 prisoners. Since crossing the Aisne River, the Guderian group claimed 250,000 prisoners in all, with thousands of pieces of vital military equipment.

By June 21 the collapse of the French armies was almost complete.

At that time, the French government was busily seeking surrender. Just after midnight, in the early hours of June 17, Paul Baudouin, the new minister of foreign affairs, called for the Spanish ambassador, and when he came to the ministry, asked him to intercede with the Germans for an armistice.

The British ambassador called on Baudouin and showed no sympathy for the French plight. The American chargé d'affaires, Anthony Drexel Biddle, called at 2:00 A.M. and was reassured that the French would never surrender their fleet to Germany. The Americans were very much concerned about this possibility, as were the British. The French gave every assurance, but still their former ally was not quite certain. Churchill sent a message to Marshal Pétain and General Weygand:

"I wish to repeat to you my profound conviction that the illustrious Marshal Pétain and the famous General Weygand will not injure their ally by delivering over to the enemy the fine French Fleet. Such an act would scarify their names for a thousand years of history. Yet this result may easily come by frittering away these few precious hours when the Fleet can be sailed to British or

American ports, carrying with it the hope and the honor of France.''

At noon on June 17, Marshal Pétain made a broadcast to France from Bordeaux in which he said, ''With a heavy heart I tell you today that it is necessary to stop the fighting.''

The French troops in the field took the marshal at face value. They quit fighting. By midafternoon General Alophonse Georges told General Weygand the marshal's broadcast had completely broken the resistance of the French army. Complete regiments refused to fight. Soldiers threw away their guns. Whole units surrendered.

The shout went up:

''The war is over. Marshal Pétain has said so. Why get killed when the war is over?'' Alongside the roads, the ditches were filled with the arms discarded by the men. In some cases commanding officers ordered their soldiers to surrender. In Brittany the Tenth Military District commander told his officers to confine the men to barracks, collect their arms, and await the arrival of the Germans. The same order was issued by the commander of the Eighteenth Military District at Bordeaux. The French military men would not even defend their new capital.

The Germans picked up the Pétain message and their propaganda teams broadcast it by loudspeaker and by leaflet. Near Cherbourg, General Rommel drove through villages in a tank waving a white flag and shouting, *''Guerre finie!''*

French troops assigned to defend Cherbourg let his column of one hundred tanks pass by without firing a shot. At Caen French and German soldiers fraternized in the cafés.

General Weygand saw the trap; Marshal Pétain had given away any bargaining power that France had left. He issued an order informing the soldiery that no armistice had been signed. But no one paid any attention to it. Admiral Darlan issued an order to the navy to hold fast, and indicated that the fleet would not be handed over to the Germans. Foreign Minister Baudouin tried to stem the tide with a clarifying message which said that Pétain had not said that the fight must stop but that they must try to stop the fighting. But it was all useless. The French had not wanted to fight, and now they were not going to fight anymore.

The British reiterated their demand for the French fleet. But nothing happened. The British Admiralty sent a message to Admiral Cunningham, commander of their Mediterranean Fleet. "If France concludes a separate peace, every effort must be employed to see that the French Fleet passes under our authority—or, if not, to sink it."

That day the United States also showed its growing distrust of the Pétain government, by freezing all French assets in the United States, a precaution against their falling into the hands of the Germans.

President Roosevelt realized that the fate of America was closely hinged to that of Britain, and that if the Germans got the French fleet, they could challenge not only the British, but they could assist the Japanese, whom America saw as their prime enemies. Further, when America entered the European war—and to Roosevelt it was a question of when, not if—the French fleet in British hands could play a positive role in the new battle for Europe. Roosevelt sent a stiff message to the French government, warning that if the French concluded an armistice and failed to keep the fleet out of German hands, such action would fatally impair the restoration of French independence, and if they surrendered the fleet to the Germans, "the French government will permanently lose the friendship and goodwill of the government of the United States."

The French were irritated by the message, but Foreign Minister Baudouin assured the American ambassador that the French fleet would never be surrendered to the Germans. It might be sent overseas or it might be scuttled, but it would not be surrendered.

In Bordeaux it was apparent to British ambassador Sir Ronald Campbell that the chances of Britain getting the French navy were minuscule. He knew that Pétain was hell-bent on surrender, and that the French were not even thinking about a time when they might fight the Germans again.

On June 18 a delegation of naval authorities from London arrived in Bordeaux to press the case for the fleet going to Britain. It included A. V. Alexander, who had replaced Churchill as First Lord of the Admiralty, Sir Dudley Pound, the first sea lord, and Lord Lloyd, the Secretary of State for Colonies, who was a personal friend of Weygand's. Lord Lloyd was a shrewd observer, and when he saw Weygand, he found him to be "a crumpled, broken, little man, completely finished and filled with vague but bitter recriminations." As for Pétain the marshal struck Lord Lloyd as "vain, senile, and dangerously ga ga." The British received many reassurances from Darlan and others, and they left not believing any of them.

Darlan then decided that the British were not to have his fleet, no matter what, and he ordered all the French ships in British ports to sail for North Africa. But the British were determined that the ships they held would not escape them, and they prevented the sailings. At Portsmouth the British admiral commanding flatly refused to allow the French to leave.

In London, General de Gaulle, with the encouragement of Prime Minister Churchill, made a broadcast to France that day, vowing to continue the fight against the Germans. But few people in France listened to it, it was accorded only a brief note in the British press, and the BBC did not even bother to make a recording of the broadcast. Not a single significant military figure offered to join De Gaulle.

In Bordeaux the government did pay attention to De Gaulle's statements, but they denied that he had any authority to make them. The new minister of war ordered the general to come home and sent a message to that effect to the French military attaché in London. De Gaulle replied that he would come home immediately if the French refused to sign the armistice. Weygand would not even reply to that message, but instead began proceedings that led soon to the court-martial of De Gaulle and his sentence in absentia to death for desertion.

At ten-thirty on the morning of June 18, an anxious Marshal Pétain broke protocol by going directly, instead of having his foreign minister go, to ask the Spanish ambassador if there had been any word yet on his request to the Germans, but there had been none. The pressure was on then for the government to move out of Bordeaux, in the face of the advancing Germans who were descending on Bordeaux. But Pétain said he would never leave France. The other ministers arranged to leave with Pétain's assent, and made their preparations to go to North Africa.

During June 18, the reason the Germans did not respond was that Hitler was meeting with Mussolini in Munich to discuss the terms of the armistice with France. The Italian attack against the French from the south had been a complete failure. After declaring war, Mussolini had sent his troops to the border, but although they outnumbered the French six to one, they made no headway at all.

"Italy's entry into the war was more of a burden to us in OKW than a relief," said General Keitel. "The führer was unsuccessful in his attempt to hold Mussolini back at least for a little while. We had a very considerable vested interest in his doing so, as for us to support their planned penetration of the French fortifications along the Alpine front would sap the strength of our own air force, and did in fact entail the dividing and weakening of our air force. Even then, despite our assistance and the weakness of the French Alpine front, the Italian offensive ground rapidly to a halt. These Italian allies of ours, who had suddenly recalled their treaty obligations to us only because they thought that France had been beaten, were to prove our most ill-starred and emptiest blessing as the war progressed, for nothing did more to impede our collaboration and entente with the French, even as early as the autumn of 1940, than our having to respect Italian aspirations and the führer's belief that we were obliged to subscribe to them.''

In the meeting at Munich, Hitler had some shocks for Mussolini. He told the Italian dictator that he did not intend to destroy France as he had destroyed Czechoslovakia. Mussolini had come north talking about Italian occupation of France and the acquisition by Italy of the French fleet. Hitler quickly disabused him of these notions. There would be no Italian occupation of France, and Italy would not get the French fleet. Hitler intended to seek agreement with the French to neutralize the fleet, to keep it out of British hands. It would be preferable that the French fleet scuttled itself, Hitler said, than that it become part of the British war effort.

Early on the morning of June 19, the Spanish ambassador appeared at Foreign Minister Baudouin's apartments with the German reply to the French request for conditions of an armistice. The first condition was that the French also sign an armistice with the Italians. The second was that the Germans receive a list of the French negotiators. A meeting was called at Marshal Pétain's office, and a panel of negotiators was chosen. None of them were top leaders of France; Weygand refused to serve since he said the Germans in 1918 had not sent their top generals to negotiate that armistice. General Charles Huntzinger was chosen to lead the delegation. He had commanded the Second French Army in the fighting around Sedan.

The French also asked that the German advance toward Bordeaux be halted. That request was passed along by the Spanish ambassador with the recommendation that it be followed because if it was not, the government at Bordeaux might collapse at any moment and the Reynaud faction, which wanted to continue the war, might gain power once more.

Later that day Foreign Minister Baudouin met the Spanish ambassador and confirmed his worst fears. If things went on as they were, he said, on June 20 the president of the republic and several other top officials were leaving for Algiers rather than be captured by the Germans.

"If Germany and Italy are interested in concluding a treaty with the French government, it appears necessary to do this as quickly as possible, and a zone must be established in which the French government can function freely and with security," the ambassador reported to Madrid, which gave the message to the German ambassador. He immediately telephoned Berlin.

On the morning of June 19, the French government was making preparations to evacuate. Admiral Darlan said the liner *Massilia* would sail from Bordeaux for Morocco at four o'clock the next afternoon. On the morning of June 20, then, all the government except Pétain was ready to go to Africa. Pétain had delegated his powers as prime minister to Vice Premier Camille Chautemps. The marshal broadcast to France again, explaining that the government was leaving but he was remaining in France. The government was preparing to leave, but at 2:00 P.M. Pétain called a special meeting of the ministers. And at that point fate, in the person of Raphael Alibert, a right-wing politician, stepped in. Alibert told President Le Brun that he had just had news that the French troops were fending off the Germans on the Loire River. It was an outright lie, fabricated to prevent the French government from leaving Bordeaux and escaping to Africa, where they might decide to continue the war. Pétain said there was no need for anyone to hurry, but President Le Brun said he was leaving anyhow. So Alibert went into another mode. He went to the office, took some of Marshal Pétain's personal stationery, and forged letters to all the ministers directing them to remain in Bordeaux until eight o'clock the next morning. He then took Pétain's personal seal, stamped the letters, and forged the marshal's signature to them. This forgery was accepted by Le Brun and others, and the *Massilia* sailed without them. Thus ended the effort of loyal Frenchmen to continue the struggle against the Germans. The defeatists and the enemies of the republic within France had won. Foreign Minister Baudouin, in meeting with Marshal Pétain, observed that President Le Brun still seemed bent on leaving Bordeaux for Africa. What would the marshal do?

"If he tries to leave," said Pétain, "I will have him arrested."

Pétain must have suspected that Le Brun was not really with him in his defeatism. In fact, Le Brun was becoming more disenchanted all the time with the Pétain government, and he suspected that Pétain was willing to accept conditions of armistice that would destroy France. If that were to happen, he intended to sack Pétain and appoint Reynaud to form a new government and continue fighting from Africa.

Pétain for his part wanted to get rid of former premier Reynaud, so he appointed him ambassador to the United States, and secured Reynaud's acceptance in principle. Pétain then sent the nomination to President Le Brun as was required by the Constitution. Le Brun, suspecting Pétain's true intent, refused to sign the nomination.

And on the afternoon of June 20, the French peace delegation left Bordeaux to meet the Germans and negotiate an armistice.

CHAPTER 6

Armistice

General Huntziger and his party left Bordeaux at two o'clock on the afternoon, bound for a certain bridge across the Loire near Tours. They had been instructed by the Germans, by telephone, to present themselves there at 5:00 P.M. They had been instructed by Marshal Pétain to break off the talks if the Germans demanded the French fleet, or the occupation of all of France, or any of the French colonies. They were also told not to sign any agreement until it had been approved by the government.

After the delegates left, Pétain and Weygand began a frantic search for copies of the armistice the French and other allies had forced on the Germans in 1918, and for the Versailles Treaty. It was in their minds that they could expect from Hitler the same sort of treatment they had meted out to the Germans twenty-two years earlier.

On their way north toward Tours, the French delegation could see the results of Marshal Pétain's unfortunate radio broadcast of June 17. They passed thousands on thousands of troops, without arms, uniforms awry, fleeing from the war front. At the moment two-thirds of France was still free of Germans, but almost all the populated places had been declared to be "open towns" and the soldiers had been ordered not to blow bridges or in any way set up a defense that would cause the towns to be destroyed.

The consequences of these actions were almost comic. The whole general staff of the Tenth French Army surrendered to a German corporal.

But the consequences were also truly tragic. France was thoroughly, miserably, defeated. The French army had completely lost its will to fight, as two illustrative cases proved. First was the case of a tank officer who insisted on defending the outskirts of the town of Vierzon against the Germans. He was killed by the people of the town, rather than have their town disturbed.

Second, even more shocking, was the case of Lieutenant Colonel Charly, who was acting commander of the remains of the Twenty-third and 153rd Artillery regiments. On the evening of June 20, the unit was encircled by the Germans at the village of Tantimont. The colonel ordered his men to attack and fight their way out of the trap. His officers and men rebelled, and angry words were said in a confrontation in an orchard on the outskirts of the village. Several of the men and officers had heard Marshal Pétain's broadcast and they refused to obey the colonel's order. Charly became angry and accused them of cowardice.

Suddenly a shot rang out and Colonel Charly fell dead.

He had been killed by a French gunner named Fernand Buret.

Here was Buret's excuse:

"On June 20 some of our officers said to the colonel, 'If we now fire a single cannon, we will all be massacred.' The colonel answered, 'The first who refuses to obey, I'll blow his brains out.' Somebody handed me a rifle, saying, 'Kill him! He's going to have us all massacred.' I fired in the direction of the colonel. I had never fired a rifle before."

So by murder and rebellion the destruction of the French army was made complete.

Observing the grisly truths as they went, the armistice delegation headed for their bridge, expecting that the talks would be conducted somewhere near Tours. But Hitler had something entirely different on his mind. For years he had virtually frothed at the mouth every time he considered the Armistice of 1918 and the Treaty of Versailles. Now, in his moment of victory, he had a chance to even the scale with Germany's ancient enemy, and he was not going to miss it.

Because the road was clogged with refugees, the automobile caravan did not reach the Loire bridge until well after dark, and there was no one to meet them but a messenger, who sent them on to Vendome, where General Kurt von Tippelskirch of the German general staff was waiting. He directed the party to go on to Chartres. The French then surmised that the Germans had selected Versailles as the meeting place. But they went from Chartres to Versailles and were then directed onward to Paris. Exhausted, they reached Paris at seven-thirty on the morning of June 21. They were taken to the Hotel Royal-Monceau, given breakfast, and told that they might rest until one-thirty in the afternoon. Then they would go on—but where, no one told them.

They found out that evening, when they drove into the Forest of Compiègne, where the railway carriage in which the 1918 Armistice had been signed had been preserved as a national monument to the victory of the Allies over the perfidious Germans of 1918. At eight-thirty that evening, General Weygand also learned. General Huntziger telephoned him.

''I'm in the wagon,'' Huntziger said. No explanation was needed. Weygand himself had sat in that wagon-lit on the night of November 10, 1918, dictating, at Marshal Foch's request, the Allied armistice terms to the Germans for the next day.

Weygand knew now what Hitler had on his mind. In fact, the Germans had taken the railroad car out of the museum that had been created to house it, by cutting out one wall of the museum, and then pushing the car along the rusty tracks to the siding where it had stood in 1918.

It all became crystal-clear to Weygand with those few words.

"Mon pauvre ami," said Weygand.

It was true, the French were calling from just outside the railroad car. They had arrived at this little place called Rethondes at around 3:00 P.M. Hitler had come at 3:15, followed by the German members of the armistice team, Marshal Goering, General Brauchitsch, Grand Admiral Raeder, Rudolph Hess, and General Wilhelm Keitel. Hitler walked up to the marble block that marked the spot where the wagon-lit had stood in 1918. He read the inscription.

"Here on the eleventh of November, 1918, succumbed the criminal pride of the German empire . . . Vanquished by the free people which it tried to enslave."

As the world press and newsreel cameramen looked on, Hitler gazed at the block with hatred, with contempt, and finally with a triumphant smile. Then he climbed into the wagon-lit, and his followers climbed in after him. Hitler sat at the center of the table, and General Keitel sat beside him. Goering sat on Hitler's other side, and the others ranged themselves alongside the two. The French followed. They sat down on the other side of the table, opposite Hitler, Keitel, and Goering. Hitler asked Keitel to read the document. General Keitel, as chief of OKW and thus Hitler's principal aide, read first a long peroration which was written by Hitler, recalling all the evils done the German people by the end of World War I and the Versailles Treaty.

"This place was selected for the armistice meeting to efface once and for all by an act of reparative justice a memory which was not for France a glorious page of her history and which was resented by the German people as the greatest shame of all time."

The conditions of the armistice had been formulated by the OKW staff long before the receipt of Pétain's request for terms. Keitel had worked over them carefully. He had been in no hurry—that is why Pétain had to wait so long—because the Germans wanted to reach the Swiss border before granting an armistice. That is why Hitler was at such great pains to question General Guderian when Guderian said he had reached the border on June 17.

Once the date for the armistice had been fixed, Hitler announced that it would be signed in the selfsame railroad car where the ignominious defeat of Germany had been settled in 1918; and then Hitler took the draft terms and retired with them for a day. He changed the draft completely, particularly the preamble.

As Keitel spoke, Hitler listened happily, and then left the car, leaving the meeting in the hands of Keitel. Goering, Brauchitsch, Hess, and Raeder then left the car. Their places were taken by General Jodl and a staff officer of the military operations office and Minister Schmidt of the Foreign Office, who acted as interpreter.

Keitel distributed copies of the German terms, with a French translation, telling the French that the terms of the armistice were inalterable and must be accepted or rejected without change. Then Keitel read the terms of the armistice the Germans were offering the French.

General Huntziger read the twenty-four clauses. He looked up at General Keitel.

"These are hard and merciless," he said.

Keitel said nothing.

The French tried to raise some objections, but did not achieve any important changes.

They asked for an hour's time to study the terms, and when it was granted, they withdrew to a tent that had been set up nearby, where there was a telephone. General Huntziger then called Bordeaux and spoke to General Weygand. The Germans, of course, monitored the entire conversation. As Keitel said:

"As was expected, the French tried valiantly to moderate our demands, and in order to win time for the telephonic transmission of the document's text—with which they had immediately begun—they claimed that they had to obtain Marshal Pétain's decision on a number of matters. I had, of course, taken the necessary steps to ensure that we could unobtrusively listen in to their telephone conversations.''

While General Huntziger was talking to General Weygand, Marshal Keitel was talking to Hitler.

The crucial clause of the treaty concerned the fate of the French fleet. Even Marshal Pétain had decided that if the Germans demanded the fleet, the talks would be broken off. Hitler seemed to sense this, because the German demands in this regard were, as General Huntziger told Marshal Weygand on the telephone, ''better than expected.'' A few ships were to be retained in the French navy for defense of the French Empire. The remainder would be demobilized and disarmed under German or Italian supervision, and laid up in their home ports. The fleet would not be available to the Allies, but it also would not be available to the Germans.

Were the Germans sincere in this pledge? ''The German government solemnly declares to the French government that it does not intend to use for its own purposes in the war the French fleet which is in ports under German supervision. Furthermore, they solemnly and expressly declare that they have no intention of raising any claim to the French fleet at the time of conclusion of peace.''

Were the Germans to be believed? William L. Shirer, historian of Nazi Germany and the Third French Republic, indicates they were not. And it does seem remarkable that Hitler would let the issue of the French fleet pass so easily when Admiral Raeder was already wondering how he could put together the invasion fleet that Hitler wanted for the storming of England. But on the other hand, Hitler had little appreciation for navies, either his own or others. His dream of empire was of a land empire, not a far-flung sea-linked empire. So it may be that the German pledge was real. In any event, the Germans must have known of the deep-seated antipathy of the French to turning their navy over to anyone.

In the event, that particular German demand did not create trouble. The French argued that the French warships, after being disarmed, be permitted to remain in North African ports, but the Germans refused the request.

Keitel felt that the Germans made certain concessions regarding the disarmament of the French air force. But there were very few concessions; Keitel spoke of "my uncompromising attitude."

One clause provided that the French turn over to the Germans all anti-Nazi German refugees, thousands of whom had fled to France in the months since the pogrom initiated by Dr. Goebbels on Kristalnacht in 1938 had shown the uncompromising hatred of the Nazis for Jews and dissenters. Weygand protested that this clause was contrary to honor, because it violated the right of asylum. The Germans refused to budge. Keitel said that this article applied to "the greatest of warmongers, the German émigrés who had betrayed their own people." The answer was no. The clause would not be eliminated.

Another article forbade the French to fight against Germany in the service of another state. The French agreed to treat such people as guerrillas, to be shot on capture. The clause was aimed at General de Gaulle, who was organizing the Free French in Britain and North Africa. But Pétain and Weygand had no sympathy for De Gaulle; soon enough he would be sentenced to death in absentia by a French court-martial.

The French were out of the war, in France and in the colonies. The armed forces would be disarmed except for a few units to maintain order. Forty percent of metropolitan France was to be left free of occupation, which meant that sixty percent would be occupied by the Germans. The Atlantic coast of France was totally occupied—in fact, it was being occupied as the talks went on—and the Germans were preparing to move the U-boat bases to France. In a sense, these bases were the most valuable assets gained by the Germans for their war effort.

The French commissioners argued as much as they dared. At five o'clock in the afternoon Keitel issued them an ultimatum. It would expire at six o'clock. If the French had not decided to accept the conditions by that time, the Germans would break off the negotations. When the French heard this, they withdrew again, telephoned to Bordeaux again, and at a few minutes after six o'clock, General Huntziger announced that they had been authorized to sign the papers.

When the ceremonies were over, Keitel dismissed all the others and held a brief talk with Huntziger. The latter was shocked to learn that the armistice with Germany would not go into effect until the French had also signed an armistice with the Italians. He pointed out that the Germans had conquered France, not the Italians. Keitel had nothing to say to that; what could he say? They all knew that Mussolini was playing the jackal's role.

The British still did not know what disposition had been made of the French fleet, and they did not find out until June 22. Then Churchill's government telegraphed Ambassador Campbell that it seemed the French government had been forced to accept terms that made it completely helpless. The only hope, said London, was Admiral Darlan, for the proposed terms put the fleet entirely at the disposal of the Germans. And who could rely on Hitler's promises? The British certainly did not intend to do so. London told the British ambassador he must insist that if the French fleet could not be surrendered to Britain or the United States, it must be scuttled.

In relying on Darlan, Churchill, the great pragmatist, was being naive. He did not realize how deep were the resentments of the French, Darlan included, against the

British for their behavior in the war. Dunkirk and the failure to commit the RAF still rankled deeply, and such men as General Weygand attributed their defeat to the British failures.

That evening of the armistice, the Germans celebrated at the führer's field headquarters. A military tattoo was held, and then the staff all sang *"Nun danket all Gott—* Now thank we all our God.'' As a good factotum, General Keitel addressed a few words of fulsome praise to Hitler as their victorious warlord, and everybody cheered. Hitler seemed to be embarrassed. He shook hands with Keitel and then left the room.

On June 22 the rupture between the two allies of two wars was virtually total. The British ambassador took his leave of Pétain that day, and of Le Brun, but not in person. They refused to see him, so he said his good-byes to Foreign Minister Baudouin. The foreign minister asked Campbell not to leave, but Campbell said he had orders from his government not to be captured by the Germans, who were approaching the estuary of the Gironde above Bordeaux. A British destroyer was waiting for him at Saint-Jean-de-Luz. So he left, and boarded the destroyer and sailed for England.

On the night of the signing, June 22, the French delegation was driven to Paris, and next day taken by German aircraft to Rome. Their next task was to negotiate an armistice with Mussolini.

In London, General de Gaulle addressed his fellow countrymen over the BBC. He called the armistice terms "not only a capitulation but an enslavement." The demobilization of the French forces would make the French totally subservient to the Germans, he said. He appealed again to all Frenchmen to join him. "The war is not lost," he said. "It is a world war."

Winston Churchill lamented the French government's acceptance of the armistice terms, and called on all Frenchmen to join the cause of Britain. Next day, an angry Marshal Pétain responded, with charges that the British had released the French from all their obligations. The fight went on.

Not one public figure in France raised his voice against the armistice. Only a lonely General de Gaulle in London talked against it, and his credentials were so poor with his colleagues that even those in London would have nothing to do with him.

While the argument about the propriety of the armistice continued in France, with virtually every politician lined up on the side of capitulation, General Huntziger and his two colleagues worked out an innocuous armistice with Italy. Mussolini was totally deflated. He would not get the French fleet. He would not get to occupy France. He had not even been given a military victory in the fighting with the French. So on the evening of June 24, 1940, the French and Italians signed an armistice, and six hours later, both armistices went into effect, as the German armistice stipulated. June 25 was proclaimed a day of mourning in France, not for the armistice, but for the 84,000 killed in forty-six days of battle, and the 120,000 wounded. The government leaders trouped to the Cathedral of Saint-Andre in Bordeaux and heard the archbishop speak of the need to ''create a New Order.''

That phrase was bandied about the capital. Pétain used it, and so did most of the other government leaders. Pierre Laval gloried in it; at last he was going to have his chance to overthrow the republic he hated so much, and the liberal politicians who had snubbed him and denied him the foreign ministry.

At the end of June, the French government moved out of Bordeaux to Clermont-Ferrand, the fief of Laval, who owned a newspaper, a radio station, a printing plant, and several other businesses. Laval had just pushed his way into the government as a minister of state. It was all Pétain's doing; Foreign Minister Baudouin cautioned against the move, and so did other of Pétain's associates, men who knew Laval's fascist tendencies, but the old marshal said it was better to have Laval in the government, where his intrigues would be less dangerous than if he were kept outside.

Immediately Pierre Laval set out to destroy the Third Republic. He announced that Marshal Pétain must be given exceptional powers, the constitution had to be revised, and the current system of political parties had to be abandoned.

When the government got to Clermont-Ferrand, Laval suggested that Pétain adjourn Parliament for six months and govern by decree. Laval wanted to get rid of President Le Brun, and the constitution and the Chamber of Deputies. Pétain told him to go ahead and try, and with this assent, Laval rushed away to begin his intrigues. As American Ambassador William Bullitt observed, the new leaders of France seemed bent on getting as far away from the old France, the democratic if corrupt France, as possible.

They wanted France to become Germany's favorite province, a new Gaul, said Bullitt.

When Bullitt talked to Marshal Pétain, he learned what was really on the old marshal's mind; Pétain wanted to get rid of the politicians. He said he believed that the cause of the fall of France had been that reserve officers who had been educated by teachers who were "socialists and not patriots" had deserted their men and shown no fighting spirit. "A sense of courage and duty must be reintroduced into France," said the marshal.

So, as Bullitt observed, the French government was bent on knuckling under to Hitler and emulating his totalitarian regime in order to curry favor with the Germans. The decision was made to move to Vichy, a resort town far removed from the realities of French life. And there Pierre Laval set to work scheming in the first ten days of July to bring down the Third Republic forcibly, and replace it with a dictatorship under Marshal Pétain, behind which Laval himself intended to rule France, in collaboration with the Germans.

Laval's cause was given an enormous boost on July 3, when Winston Churchill acted regarding the French fleet, in the defense of his own country, without any further consideration for the old French alliance.

As for the French, they waited nervously to discover the sort of peace the Germans would force upon them, realizing that except for some particularly harsh Nazi terms, such as the demand for anti-Nazi refugees, the armistice was a copy of the one they had forced on the Germans in 1918. They did not have to wait long. Three days after the signing of the armistice, the stone marker in the Compiègne forest was blown to bits by Hitler's express order. France was in the hands of the Germans, and the French were to become slaves.

CHAPTER 7

The Fate of the Fleet; the Fate of France

At about midnight of June 22, when British Ambassador Campbell took leave of French Foreign Minister Baudouin, the French-British alliance ceased to exist. Campbell's departure "for consultation" was really the signal for complete breach of diplomatic relations. Within hours the two former allies were name-calling and scheming against each other.

As Britain's firmest advocate of French-British cooperation, Winston Churchill had done all in his power to keep France in the war, but he had failed in the face of a defeatist attitude that permeated the country—an attitude exemplified by Marshal Pétain.

Having failed, Churchill then turned to consideration of Britain's own salvation. For four days the War Cabinet debated what must be done to keep the French fleet from falling into the hands of the Germans. On June 27 they decided that the French fleet must be seized, disabled, or destroyed. They set up a plan with the Admiralty, called Operation Catapult. It was to be carried out on July 3.

The French fleet was scattered across Europe and Africa. In the British ports of Plymouth and Portsmouth lay two battleships, four light cruisers, eight destroyers, a number of submarines, and two hundred smaller craft.

At the British naval base in Alexandria, Egypt, was a whole French squadron, one battleship, four cruisers, three destroyers, a submarine, and many smaller vessels. In Algeria at Mers-el-Kebir near Oran lay the cream of the French fleet, which consisted of two battleships, the modern battle cruisers *Dunquerque* and *Strasbourg*, which outclassed the *Scharnhorst* and *Gneisenau*, because that was what they had been built to do, four light cruisers, several destroyers, and many submarines. Altogether on the African coast and off Beirut, the French had twenty-two of those invaluable destroyers, so badly needed by Britain for the antisubmarine war. In the hands of the British, they and all the other ships could be an enormous asset. In the hands of the Germans, they could mean disaster, for altogether in the Mediterranean the French had three battleships, two battle cruisers, one aircraft carrier, eleven cruisers, twenty-five destroyers, and thirty-two submarines.

Churchill agonized over the decision, which he termed "the most unnatural and painful in which I have ever been concerned," but British self-interest demanded that the French fleet not get into the hands of the German-Italian combination, and that was the deciding factor. Hitler had said he would not use the French fleet, but no responsible political leader in Britain believed him. On July 1 the British Admiralty issued an order to all fleet units to be prepared for Operation Catapult on July 3.

The admirals involved protested, Admiral Sir Andrew Cunningham, commander of the Mediterranean Fleet, and Vice Admiral Sir James Somerville, commander of Force H at Gibraltar. But Churchill was adamant; he did not believe anything Hitler said, and if Hitler said he would not take the French fleet, that meant he most certainly would take it. That fleet in German hands would give Admiral Raeder the ships necessary to make possible the invasion of Britain. So the admirals were told to keep silent and obey their orders.

Just before dawn on July 3, armed British naval patrols boarded the French ships at Plymouth, overpowered the French sailors on watch, seized the vessels, and sent the French crews ashore. Only on one submarine, the *Surcouf*, was there violence, and there one French sailor was killed and one British sailor was killed and three were wounded. At Portsmouth the operation went even more smoothly, and by sunrise all the French naval ships in British water were in British hands. The twenty thousand French sailors were given the choice: go home to France, or join General de Gaulle's Free French forces in Britain. Nearly 95 percent of them opted to return to France; only nine hundred men decided to join De Gaulle. The French navy, like the French army, did not believe in the war.

At Alexandria the French and British commanders issued specific orders that might have brought about a bloody clash. Admiral Darlan had ordered his commander, Admiral Rene Godfroy, to fight his way out of the harbor with his battleship, four cruisers, and three destroyers. Admiral Cunningham was told to issue an ultimatum to the French to give up, sink their ships, or be destroyed. But instead Admiral Cunningham talked, and in the end the French agreed to dump their fuel oil, remove parts of the ships' guns so they could not fire, and accept temporary internment and repatriation. At Alexandria there was no trouble.

At Mers-el-Kebir, however, the story was not the same. This was a French naval base, and when Admiral Somerville's Force H appeared at 9:00 A.M. on July 3, Admiral Gensoul decided to fight. Somerville sent in to shore Captain Cedric Swinton Holland, in the destroyer *Foxhound*, to talk to the French. Captain Holland was well-known to the French, having served as naval attaché at Paris, and he was well liked as well. But the message he brought, composed by Churchill, was not welcome to the French. It told them they had three alternatives: to join the British and fight the Germans, to sail their ships to a British port and give them up, or to sail with British escort to some French port in the West Indies or to the United States. Otherwise they must scuttle the ships within six hours, or the British would destroy them with gunfire and bombing.

Admiral Gensoul replied that force would be met with force, and he so telegraphed Darlan. But he did not mention the alternatives, and particularly the one that appealed to many in the French government, the alternative of sailing to a French port in the New World.

The French prepared for action, but they were at a disadvantage. Their battleships were moored together, making a big target, but they were unable to maneuver and make full use of their guns. Half the crews were on shore leave. Some of the guns had been dismantled to meet the demands of the Germans in the armistice. Also, the Germans were informed of the ultimatum, and the response. The new ally was more important to the French than the old one.

General Huntziger apologized to the Germans for violating the terms of the armistice by planning to fight the British. Hitler was informed and he could not have been more pleased. He responded personally to Huntziger, telling him that the terms of the armistice were suspended as far as North Africa was concerned and that the French could quite properly turn their guns on the British.

Aboard the French flagship *Dunquerque*, Captain Holland and Admiral Gensoul talked all afternoon. The admiral was playing for time, while his men put their warships back into fighting trim. Holland was carrying out a mission that was personally distasteful to him, but he did so punctiliously. Talk, talk, talk. Gensoul insisted that he had made preparations to be sure his ships did not fall into German hands, and he showed the captain a message from Admiral Darlan instructing him to scuttle his ships at the first sign of a German demand to take over. But Holland knew how easy it had been for the British to take the French ships in British harbors, although the French had known that it was going to happen. They had not been quick enough to stop it. Gensoul offered to disarm his ships and gave his personal word of honor that if the ships were menaced, he would sail them to the West Indies. Holland reported this offer back to the *Hood*, where Admiral Somerville's flag flew.

"This is not quite our proposition. Can get no nearer."

But that was not satisfactory to Admiral Somerville. He sent a message to the French admiral:

"If one of our propositions is not accepted by 5:30 P.M. British summer time, I shall have to sink your ships."

In London, Churchill was following the exchange of messages, and he realized that the British officers were most reluctant to act against their former ally. He sent a message to Somerville telling him, "French ships must comply with our terms or sink themselves or be sunk by you before dark."

By the time that Admiral Somerville received that message, he was already in action. At 5:54 P.M. the British destroyers offshore had laid a smoke screen, and the British fleet opened fire on the French with their big guns. Planes from the carrier *Ark Royal* flew over and bombed the French. Fifteen minutes later, it was all over. The *Bretagne* blew up and sank. The battleship *Provence* and the *Dunquerque* were both badly damaged and beached. The battle cruiser *Strasbourg* escaped, crippled by several salvos, and made her way to Toulon. On the way she was further damaged from air attack. In all, the French lost three capital ships and a number of smaller vessels. Nearly 1,300 French sailors died, and 341 were wounded. Damage to the British ships was minor, and very few men were killed or wounded.

The reaction in London was cheers for the War Cabinet that had acted so resolutely. The reaction in France was horror and resentment against a former ally that had stabbed France in the back. In Vichy, Pierre Laval and Admiral Darlan called for a declaration of war against Britain. Admiral Darlan called on the French cruiser squadron, which had escaped from Oran, to attack Admiral Somerville's squadron. When a horrified Foreign Minister Baudouin exclaimed, "Why, that means war!" Marshal Pétain simply assented. But the French cabinet, meeting on July 4, accepted Baudouin's proposal that diplomatic relations be formally broken, but that no war be declared.

The end result of the action against the French fleet was to unify the French people in hatred of England, and turn their feelings away from the Germans for the moment. Pierre Laval took advantage of this feeling to propose that the National Assembly meet on July 10 and abolish the 1875 Constitution of the Third Republic.

Laval was now ready to act to seize power. He was a man of his time, who had begun in World War I as a left-wing socialist, but who had moved steadily to the right of the political spectrum and now found Fascism and Nazism most appealing. He held deep resentments against the liberal politicians, who had kept him out of office since 1936, he who had been prime minister of conservative governments three times in the past. Now, with the support of the man journalist William Shirer saw as "the doddering Marshal Pétain," who admitted he knew nothing about politics and cared less, Laval sought power again. He was almost alone among the political leaders of the French government, who knew exactly what he wanted.

As Vincent Auriol, one of Laval's enemies, characterized him, "Everything about him is black: his clothes, his face, his soul."

Laval set about organizing the Parliamentarians, in the confusion of his enemies, like Paul Reynaud, who had been injured in an auto accident. He held Marshal Pétain virtually prisoner, not letting him meet with rival political leaders, turning them away through Raphael Alibert, counselor to Pétain, who arranged his appointments. Laval spread a rumor that if the Parliamentarians did not accept his proposals, the government would be taken over by General Weygand in a military coup. The scared political leaders began to flock to him.

Laval spoke with brutal frankness in Parliament. "We are going to destroy the totality of what was. We are going to create something entirely different. Either you accept what we demand and align yourself with a German or Italian constitution, or Hitler will impose it on you. Henceforth there will be only one party, that of all the French."

He now proposed that Pétain be made the dictator of France. Many agreed, but Georges Monnet, a socialist, asked, if something happened to Pétain, who would succeed him?

"The marshal himself will name his successor," said Laval. And he worked unceasingly on the marshal to be sure that the person named was going to be Pierre Laval.

Laval confided in Foreign Minister Baudouin that he wished to appear in the eyes of the National Assembly to be the man designated by the marshal to carry out the constitutional reform if anything should happen to Pétain. General Weygand would be designated as second in line. Baudouin then went to Pétain, who showed very little enthusiasm for Laval, and they agreed that Weygand was the man.

But Laval continued to lobby for himself. His first task was to get Pétain made dictator. But some of the staunch republican deputies opposed the handing over of power to anyone. They called on Pétain and expressed their fears. He assured them that he had no desire to be dictator. If they gave him power, he said, he would use it in the open, and he would govern only until peace was made with Germany, at which time he would retire. The deputies were much relieved, and they believed the marshal when he said, "I am not a Caesar, nor do I wish to be." They assured him that they were willing to give him every power to maintain order and reestablish and reconstitute the country and conclude the peace. Both sides retired, each much satisfied with the other.

The next day the senators offered Pétain a proposition providing for suspension of the constitution, giving the marshal all power to govern by decree and prepare a new constitution in consultation with the legislative committees, which would then be ratified by the nation in an election. He liked it, but Laval did not, and by intrigue, Laval triumphed.

On July 9 at 9:30 in the morning, the Chamber of Deputies met at the Grand Casino (which they used as Parliament in the morning, while the Senate used it in the afternoon) and voted to wipe out the Third Republic and give Pétain dictatorial power. Even the name "Republic" was to be abandoned. In secret session on the morning of June 10, the National Assembly made preparations to put itself out of office, and at 2:00 P.M. that day, in public session, it did so.

"The National Assembly," the motion read, "gives all powers to the government of the republic under the authority and signature of Marshal Pétain to promulgate by one or several acts a new constitution of the French state. This constitution will guarantee the rights of work, family, and country. It will be ratified by the nation and applied by the assemblies which it will create."

It was apparent that Pierre Laval had taken control when he rammed two motions through the Assembly. One removed the quorum requirement. Votes could be carried by a majority of those on the floor, not a majority of the membership. The other was the vote on the government resolution, which was rammed through without any hearing for the opposition.

So on the afternoon of July 10, the vote was called,

and 569 members voted to turn the government into a totalitarian state run by Marshal Pétain, while 80 voted against it and 17 members abstained. The Third Republic died. Three days later, President Le Brun stepped down and Pétain took over. France fell into the hands of the fascists.

CHAPTER 8

Operation Sea Lion

With the fall of France, the attention of the British and the Germans was turned to the same subject: invasion by the Germans of the British Isles.

As Prime Minister Churchill put the matter:

"We are greatly concerned—and it is certainly wise to be so—with the dangers of the German landing in England in spite of our possessing the command of the seas and having very strong defense by fighters in the air. Every creek, every beach, every harbor has become to us a source of anxiety. Besides this, the parachutists may sweep over and take Liverpool or Ireland and so forth."

But Churchill refused to get bogged down in a defensive mentality. This, he said, was what had destroyed France. Certainly defense against invasion was very much on his mind, but so was such offensive action as Britain might take.

"It is of the highest consequence to keep the largest numbers of German forces all along the coasts of the countries they have conquered, and we should immediately set to work to organize raiding forces on these coasts where the populations are friendly."

Churchill's inquiring mind was turning over the whole matter of keeping the Germans off balance, and out of this would come a very active role for the Special Operations Executive, which he put under the Ministry of

Economic Warfare under Hugh Dalton that month of July 1940. Dalton had the same idea:

"We must organize movements in enemy-occupied territory compared to the Sinn Fein movement in Ireland, to the Chinese guerrillas now operating against Japan, to the Spanish Irregulars in Wellington's campaign. We must use many different methods, including industrial and military sabotage, labor agitation and strikes, continuous propaganda, terrorist acts against traitors and German leaders . . ." said Dalton.

All this was a part of Churchill's determination to shake off the lassitude of moral prostration that he saw around him in the paralysis that followed Dunkirk.

Out of this Churchillian musing would come the establishment of the "commandos" and the Combined Operations Command under Sir Roger Keyes, the landing craft Tank (LCT), and other elements of warfare germinated in that fertile Churchillian brain.

But in another area of his mind, Churchill was greatly concerned with the possibility of German invasion, particularly since the British fleet had not truly destroyed the French fleet despite what happened at Mers-el-Kebir, and at Portsmouth and other British harbors. The large remainder of the French fleet lay in Toulon, where it had to be regarded as hostage to the Germans, potentially dangerous in the invasion of Britain.

The French surrender had given the Germans enormous confidence. General Jodl, chief of operations of OKW, said on June 30, "The final German victory over England is now only a matter of time." Hitler had already ordered a partial demobilization of the German army, calling for a cut from 160 divisions to 120 divisions. The assumption was that the struggle against England could now be carried on by the navy and the Luftwaffe. Reich Minister Hermann Goering told Hitler that the navy was not necessary to defeat England; his air force could do it single-handedly.

In July, now that the challenge was obvious, decisions had to be made. What was Germany's course now to be? Hitler had been thoroughly preoccupied with the battle in the West, so much so that he paid little attention to considerations of overall war strategy. Admiral Raeder had kept reminding him that there were ways of striking at England, in the Mediterranean and elsewhere. One of the considerations that spring and summer had been a possible invasion of the British islands, as Churchill feared, and when Hitler offered his "olive branch" after the fall of France and the British spurned him, he was stung to the point of fury, and wanted nothing so much as to bring Britain to her knees.

In November 1939 Admiral Raeder had told his planning staff to consider the thought of invading the British Isles. The idea of invading Britain had been discussed within the army and the Luftwaffe high commands in the fall and winter of 1939–40. The army offered a plan, but the navy and air force rejected it in January 1940 as unrealistic. The navy said the plan did not show any understanding of British naval power. The Luftwaffe said the plan did not show any understanding of the strength of the British Royal Air Force.

When it became apparent in mid-May that the German drive through Belgium and France was succeeding beyond the expectations of the army high command, Admiral Raeder began to think seriously about the next steps. When the panzers drove through to Abbeville and the seas, cutting off the Allied armies, Raeder had some idea. The next day, May 21, Raeder held a private conversation with Hitler in which he brought up the possibility. Hitler was noncommittal, his mind was on the battle before him.

But the navy general staff continued to study the problems of invasion of Britain. On May 27 Rear Admiral Kurt Fricke, chief of the Operations Division, brought forth a new study of the invasion idea. The big problem was the provision of landing craft and adequate shipping to take the invasion force across the English Channel. Germany was not equipped for amphibious operations. Many ideas were bandied about, including the invention of a "war crocodile," a barge made of ferroconcrete, which would be cheap, easy to build, and could carry a company of two hundred men with their equipment or several tanks and artillery pieces. This was the sort of thinking Hitler always liked; new weapons intrigued him. On June 20 he discussed the idea with General Halder and Admiral Raeder, but nothing very definitive was said. One reason for that indecision was the enormous optimism generated by the easy victories. The men around Hitler fully expected, as did the French, that the British would now give up the battle. So why talk about something that probably was not going to be necessary?

Hitler was at the moment bemused with victory. On June 21 Hitler appeared at Compiègne in the wagon-lits where the armistice with France was worked out, but then went off on a tour of World War I battlefields where he had served. After the signing of the armistice on June 24, Hitler and the new Field Marshal Keitel made a trip to Paris. They took off in a plane from Berlin at 4:00 A.M. and landed at Le Bourget airfield two hours later, before Paris had begun to pull itself together for the day. They drove up to Montmartre and looked out over the city, and then visited the Arc de Triomphe and the Eiffel Tower. Hitler insisted on going to the Opera, whose internal architecture he had studied in his Vienna days. He also visited Napoleon's tomb. In the company was Albert Speer, Hitler's architect, who was now told that he must make of Berlin a city superior to Paris in every way. So obviously Hitler's mind was not just then on the problems of dealing with a Britain that he did not really expect to be recalcitrant in view of the German victory.

But on June 18 Winston Churchill reiterated in the

House of Commons Britain's "inflexible resolve to continue the war," and not long afterward when the king of Sweden urged Britain to accept a peace settlement, Churchill told him grimly, "Before any such requests or proposals could even be considered, it would be necessary that effective guarantees by deeds, not words, should be forthcoming from Germany which would insure the restoration of the free and independent life of Czechoslovakia, Poland, Norway, Denmark, Holland, Belgium, and above all, France."

But in Germany in this period, everyone expected peace to come. William L. Shirer, the journalist, recalled those summer days "where everyone, especially in the Wilhelmstrasse and the Bendlerstrasse, was confident that the war was as good as over." On July 1 Hitler told the new Italian ambassador, Dino Alfieri, that he could not conceive of anyone in Britain still believing in possible victory. But the next day, in the absence of any specific actions, Hitler took the first tentative steps toward invasion of his enemy's country. OKW issued a mild statement of intent, if he had air superiority, and if "certain other conditions are fulfilled." No date for carrying out the plan was set.

On July 11 Hitler met with Admiral Raeder to discuss the matter of the possible invasion. Raeder was not keen on it at the moment, because he did not have the ships to transport the troops. He suggested that the air force be used to subdue the British and bring them to terms. That action, along with the increase in submarine activity, should do the job. Hitler came away from that meeting convinced that the problems of invasion were indeed severe. But for once he was getting pressure from the German army for action. As Field Marshal Keitel put it:

"Nobody feared the British army since its collapse and its enormous material losses at Dunkirk, but the Royal Air Force and the vastly superior Royal Navy were factors which could not be ignored. The War Office was therefore accordingly strongly in favor of risking the operation and made every possible effort to promote its execution; for the first time Hitler found himself under considerable pressure from that quarter, a circumstance to which he was totally unaccustomed.''

Goering was confident of his Luftwaffe—he exuded overconfidence, in fact. But Raeder kept talking about the shortage of landing craft, and of the trouble of supply and antiaircraft defense, as well as providing a screen against the superior British navy. Another problem: they would have to use Rhine River barges and canal boats from Belgium and Holland as landing craft, and the damage of the war to the canal locks and waterways had forced the closure of large parts of the waterway system.

And, as the army began to realize, all these craft had to be adjusted for landing of tanks and artillery, and equipped with antiaircraft guns and with engines to let them move under their own power.

Hitler persisted in his optimism about the peaceful solution during the early days of July. But by July 13, when his generals came to Berchtesgaden aerie for a meeting, the optimism was fading. He told them that he could not understand why the British did not accept the olive branch of peace that he offered them, not realizing yet that Churchill would never accept one word of Hitler's as truth.

But after the meeting with the generals, Hitler began to talk in a different manner. He had decided that Churchill was pinning his hopes on the Russians, and if this was the case, then Britain would have to be compelled by more force to make peace. He did not like the idea of smashing the British Empire, for it would not help Germany at all, but would profit the United States and Japan only, he said.

He had grown disgusted with the negative British attitude, and said he was convinced that the British would never listen until they were forced to do so by another military defeat. On July 13 he issued Directive No. 15 for the conduct of the air war, calling for the offensive against Britain to begin on August 5. On July 16 he issued the operational orders for Operation Sea Lion, but the feeling in OKW was still tentative. On July 19 he spoke to the *Reichstag* again, making his "final" peace offer to Churchill. He was very impressive in the confidence of his recent victory, but he pretended a humility he did not feel, and the effect was very powerful on the German people, if not on the British. He was controlled for a change—no shouting—as he insulted Churchill and twisted the facts of recent history. Admiral Raeder counseled for taking the war to the Mediterranean, capturing Gibraltar. But at the moment Hitler was not listening. He was still looking for a quick victory over Britain. And Hermann Goering seemed to promise it to him. Goering spoke loftily of bringing the British to heel with the use of the Luftwaffe alone.

General Jodl of OKW prepared a paper outlining a strategy for the future. It was entitled "The Continuation of the War Against England." The first step, said Jodl, should be the intensification of the air war. This should be accompanied by a step-up in the U-boat war. "Together with propaganda and periodic terror attacks, announced as reprisal, this increased weakening of the basis of the food supply will paralyze and finally break the will of the people to resist, and thereby force the government to capitulate."

The principle was sound enough, and no one recognized that more clearly than Winston Churchill, who gave what some thought was inordinate attention to the anti-submarine war. But Churchill was ever mindful of the slenderness of the lifeline of Britain to the colonies and the New World.

The army general staff allocated thirteen divisions for the first wave of the invasion, and produced a plan for a landing on the south coast of England. Field Marshal von Rundstedt would carry the battle with Army Group A. Six divisions of the Sixteenth Army would sail from the Pas de Calais and land on beaches from Ramsgate to Bexhill. Four divisions of the Ninth Army would leave Le Havre and cross the Channel to land between Brighton and the Isle of Wight. Farther west would land three divisions of the Sixth Army coming from the Cherbourg peninsula. They would land in Lyme Bay between Weymouth and Lyme Regis.

This was the first wave—90,000 men. By the third day, the Germans would have ashore 260,000 men, plus airborne forces who would be dropped inshore of Lyme Bay. These troops would be followed by six panzer divisions and three motorized divisions, and within ten days, the Germans would have thirty-nine divisions and two airborne divisions ashore in England.

The initial objective was to establish the bridgeheads, then move inland as rapidly as possible, with Army Group A taking a line that ran between Gravesend and Southampton. The Sixth Army would advance north to Bristol, cutting off Devon and Cornwall from the rest of England. The third objective would be a line between Maldon on the east coast, north of the Thames Estuary, and to the Severn River, thus blocking off Wales. London would be surrounded, and the northward drive resumed. The whole operation would be finished in a month, Brauchitsch told Admiral Raeder.

Raeder looked over the plans. It was obvious that they had been drawn by military men who were used to fighting on land, and not at sea. The initial front would stretch more than two hundred miles, from Ramsgate to Lyme Bay. How could the German navy, far inferior to the British, protect the troops from sea and air attack? There was no way, there were not nearly enough ships or men. So said Raeder to the army, and on July 21 he also told Hitler that the plan was unworkable. Hitler had summoned Raeder to meet with Brauchitsch and Hans Jechonnek, the chief of the Luftwaffe general staff. He seemed to believe that Raeder's difficulties were more apparent than real, and he seemed also to be gathering enthusiasm for the operation. He would not press, he said, but the war must be ended as soon as possible. He would like to have it all sewed up by September 15.

The army men agreed with him. If the navy would carry them to England, they would win, they said. British army strength, by German estimate, was eight divisions. Actually, there were twenty-nine divisions in England at this time, but only about half of them were properly armed and equipped. By the middle of September, however, Churchill planned to have sixteen divisions, three of them armored, in the south, and four divisions and an armored brigade covering the east coast. Immense American assistance, undreamed-of by the Germans, made this remarkable recovery possible in such a short time after the Dunkirk debacle.

But the big problem of the British, at this point, was that they had no way of knowing what the Germans were up to. The debacle in France had wiped out their intelligence organization on the continent, and it was going to take time to rebuild. In the summer of 1940 the British intelligence estimates about German plans were almost totally inaccurate. They believed the Germans planned their main landings on the east coast, south of London, when the precise opposite was true. Therefore, the British divisions were being concentrated in the East.

Raeder did not believe the German army projections and he renewed his objections. To face the British navy was bad enough, but to also face the Royal Air Force, an unknown quantity but reputedly very strong, was twice as bad. Raeder asked for more time and more information.

Hitler still believed the war was virtually over and he told General Halder just this. "The war has been won by us. A reversal of the prospects of success is impossible.''

By July 29 the German naval general staff had concluded that it would be impossible to mount the invasion in 1940 and suggested that it be delayed.

But Hitler wanted to tidy up his world, and convinced as he was that all the British needed was a good push to get them out of the war, he called his chief military leaders together again on July 31 at his house at Obersalzberg. Field Marshal Keitel and General Jodl were there from OKW, and Brauchitsch and Halder from the army general staff. They had come to listen to Admiral Raeder put his case against Operation Sea Lion.

Raeder faced many problems, not the least of which was his knowledge that Hitler really wanted to go ahead. The operation could not be launched until September 15 at the earliest, he said, and even then it would depend on good weather, and what the British did. Weather, that was a big problem.

Hitler asked questions about the weather, and Raeder was prepared with eloquent answers and figures. The weather in the English Channel in the fall was usually very bad. The first two weeks of October might be fair, but after that, it would be fog and choppy water, and the choppiness was the worst part, because the Rhine barges and other craft that could be converted to be landing craft were not very stable, and likely to sink in rough water. If they sank, then what would the ships do to unload their supplies?

The problem (which the Allies faced four years later) was that the Channel weather was basically unstable. If the first wave crossed successfully, that did not mean the second and third waves would have such luck. Indeed, they could expect from the record that after the first wave crossed, there would be a hiatus of several days.

Another problem, Raeder said, was that the army wanted too broad a front for its operations, from the

Dover strait to Lyme Bay. To meet these requirements, to land one hundred thousand men in the first wave along a two hundred mile front, would mean the navy must provide 1,700 barges, 1,100 motorboats, 470 tugs, and 150 transports. To do this would absolutely strip the German home economy of water transport. And then there was the problem of protecting the fleet against the attacks of the RAF and the Royal Navy. The navy did not have the resources to manage it; the front should run from Dover Strait to Eastbourne. The generals listened to that appraisal in silence; shortening the front might make it easier for the navy, but it made life more iffy for the army. One of the best features of their plan, they believed, was its widespread nature, which would prevent the British from concentrating their defensive power.

And what, then, did Admiral Raeder propose?

He proposed that the invasion be delayed and attempted at the time of year the weather was best in the English Channel, a delay that would also give the navy a chance to strengthen its amphibious capability. And when was that?

May 1941, said Admiral Raeder. If there was to be action in the fall, it should be in the Mediterranean, where the British could be struck some powerful blows, and where Germany had the Italian army and navy to work with.

Hitler did not like it. Of course, they could not do anything about the weather, he admitted, but other factors militated against delay. The German navy would not be any stronger in the spring (except in U-boats) than it was in the fall of 1940. The British army had been decimated in France, but Britain had the manpower, and in ten months it would have rebuilt its army to thirty to thirty-five divisions.

It was all very well to talk about diversionary activity in Africa, but the fact was, Hitler said, that Britain would have to be hit at home to knock her out of the war. Therefore, the plans for the invasion should go ahead, aiming at September 15, 1940. Marshal Goering had assured Hitler that he could knock out the British air force, and that was the key. Goering was to make a concentrated attack on the south of England for one week. If the attacks succeeded in breaking the back of the Royal Air Force, then Operation Sea Lion would proceed. If Goering failed, then the operation would be postponed until the spring of 1941.

The meeting broke up on that note.

Next day, Hitler issued his war Directive No. 17.

Führer's Headquarters
August 1, 1940

Top Secret

DIRECTIVE NO. 17
FOR THE CONDUCT OF AIR AND NAVAL WAR-
FARE AGAINST ENGLAND

In order to establish the conditions necessary for the final conquest of England, I intend to continue the air and naval war against the English homeland more intensively than heretofore.

TO THIS END I ISSUE THE FOLLOWING ORDERS:

1. The German air force is to overcome the British air force with all means at its disposal and as soon as possible.

2. After gaining temporary or local air superiority, the air war is to be carried out against harbors, especially against establishments connected with food supply.

3. Attacks on the harbors of the south coast are to be undertaken on the smallest scale possible in view of our intended operations.

4. The Luftwaffe is to stand by for Operation Sea Lion.

5. I reserve for myself the decision on terror attacks as a means of reprisal.

6. The intensified air war may commence on or after August 6. The navy is authorized to begin the projected intensified naval warfare at the same time.

(Signed)
Adolf Hitler

That same day Field Marshal Keitel promulgated orders alerting the air force and the navy to their responsibilities under the plan for Operation Sea Lion. Nothing had changed in Hitler's mind. The front would be as broad as the army wanted. The air force would be ready, and so would the navy, on September 15. Only one loophole was left:

"Eight to fourteen days after the launching of the air offensive against Britain, scheduled to begin about August 5, the führer will decide whether the invasion will take place this year or not; his decision will depend largely on the outcome of the air offensive."

The feud between army and navy grew sharper, because of the army's insistence on the broad front. And that insistence was based on a misreading of the power of the British defenses. German intelligence about Britain was virtually nonexistent. All the German agents had been rounded up at the outset of the war, and throughout the war, the only "agents" the *Abwehr* and other intelligence agencies were able to contact in England were plants by the British. So the German general staff had a highly overblown idea of Britain's strength, which was helped along by selective British propaganda about the country's growing strength.

Marshal Goering had moved his headquarters to Paris for the forthcoming assault against England, and he had sent his personal armored train to Calais, where it was parked near a tunnel in a siding. He commuted between the two, enjoying the delights of Paris as he worried about the problems of his Luftwaffe. The actual operations were directed by Generals Milch and Jeschonnek. Goering's role was to deal with Hitler, and he spent much of his time on the telephone to the führer's headquarters.

As General Milch and General Jeschonnek knew very well, the Luftwaffe was hardly constituted to perform the task that Goering so lightheartedly accepted. What was wanted to win the air battle of Britain was a preponderance of fighters and bombers, the fighters to engage the enemy fighters, while the bombers destroyed the air force capability. But Germany did not have any heavy bombers, because before 1939, the air force mission had been seen as support of army operations, and for this task, the Stuka dive-bombers and twin-engined medium bombers were ideal.

As of July 1, the Luftwaffe had 725 single-engine fighters in service, while the RAF had only 644. But Marshal Goering was again the victim of poor intelligence. General Josef Schmid, his chief of intelligence, estimated that the Luftwaffe, as of July, was clearly superior to the RAF in every category. Britain was credited with a capacity to build only 180 first-line fighters per month, and only 150 bombers. Actual British fighter production then was nearly 500, and production was rising. The Germans were producing at about half that rate. So no special measures were taken to boost production either of fighter planes or of bombers. As a consequence, fighter production in Germany was actually decreasing. British fighter plane production was 43 percent ahead of planning, while German fighter production was 40 percent behind.

The preliminary campaign began in mid-July. After the fall of France, Admiral Doenitz insisted on support from the Luftwaffe for submarine operations, and a long-range reconnaissance unit I./KG.40—the First Gruppe of the Fortieth Bomber Squadron, at full strength thirty aircraft, was assigned to do reconnaissance for the U-boats.

Meanwhile, although Germany did not have any agents in Britain, they thought they did, and instructed these people to begin sending weather reports. Their British masters played along with the game.

The Luftwaffe began attacking ships in the English Channel and sank a number of ships that were not traveling in convoy. On July 10 what the British reckoned to be the beginning of the intensive air campaign began when the Luftwaffe put seventy planes over dock targets in South Wales ports. There were losses on both sides—nothing definitive.

Between July 11 and July 24, the Luftwaffe made many attacks on shipping in the Channel. They quickly discovered two salient facts: The Stuka dive-bomber might have been satisfactory for attacks on troops, but against shipping and port facilities, it was a sitting duck—too slow. Also, the ME–109 fighter plane was outmatched by the British Spitfire. At the end of the two weeks, plane losses were forty-eight for the RAF and ninety-three for the Luftwaffe.

Meanwhile, sensing that there was some special meaning in the German stepping up of attacks on shipping, the British took note and redoubled their efforts at home defense. A thousand armed patrol craft coursed the waters around England, and behind them were the flotillas of destroyers: 1,140 destroyers disposed between the Humber River and Portsmouth, with most of them going to sea every night, and the others patrolling by day. It was expected that no matter where the Germans landed, these ships would get there within an hour or two and start breaking up the landing craft. This made it essential that the ships have fighter protection during the daylight hours, and this was one of the reasons the British never relaxed their vigilance in the matter of aircraft construction. They felt the need for more and more aircraft.

In Parliament someone asked the question: What would the Royal Navy do if the Germans covered the landings in England with their heavy warships?

The answer: Because of the vigilance of the Home Fleet and the RAF in the past, there were no heavy German units available for action. Two big ships, the *Bismarck* and the *Tirpitz*, were building, but they were not built. And all of the ships available to the Germans at the outset of the war had been sunk or damaged, the *Scharnhorst* and *Gneisenau* in Norwegian waters, the *Graf Spee* sunk in the River Plate, and all the others hurt one way or the other in the naval actions of the past few months. As far as strength was concerned, Britain had plenty and to spare in heavy ships for any moves the Germans might want to make. The Thames and Humber rivers were full of cruisers, strong enough to take care of any light cruisers the Germans might send with an invasion flotilla. So Winston Churchill did not believe the Germans would be able to move to the east coast of England. But he neglected his homework on the question of the south and west of England, where the Germans were planning to make their invasion attempt. He passed this off with the comment that no great mass of shipping existed in French ports, and that the number of small boats there was not great. He did not understand that the Germans were really starting from scratch, but they were about to start assembling the invasion fleet. But Churchill did see that there was danger from Dover to the Wash, from the Dutch and German harbors, about which he knew very little. And he knew far better than Hitler did of vagaries of Channel weather in the autumn of the year, so he was not particularly concerned.

What bothered Churchill most in July was the fact that too many of the British troops were lining up around the shores, looking nervously seaward for invasion attempts, and not training for the major effort. He asked General Ismay to bring them back to camps, and get on with the training and stop looking over their shoulders.

The British problem was to prepare against all eventualities, as Churchill put it, "and yet at the same time avoid the dispersion of our mobile forces and to gather reserves." The only way they could do this was to keep track of news and events from week to week. They watched the Channel ports for signs of activity, they watched the Bay of Biscay, and they watched Germany proper.

With a two-thousand-mile coastline to defend, the British evolved a plan calling for lines of resistance around the coast, where Home Guards and others would delay the enemy. Meanwhile the British army trained a huge mass of troops and assured their mobility so they could be thrown against any point of attack very quickly. This plan was a result of Churchill's observation in France, when the battle had been going badly, but was not yet lost. Noting the breakthrough at Abbeville, on one of his trips to meet with the French, Churchill had asked, "*Et, où est la masse de manoeuvre?*" to be told ruefully by General Gamelin that the French had no reserves. The failure to provide them had cost the Allies the battle of France, and cost the British Expeditionary Force almost all its equipment and supplies. It was not a mistake Churchill was likely to repeat in Britain.

In the first week of August, the basic defense plan was laid. The RAF and the Royal Navy's submarines were keeping a close watch on the enemy shore, from the Baltic to the Spanish border with France. Destroyers and other craft patrolled day and night along the shores. RAF and Royal Navy were prepared to attack the enemy the moment he appeared in British waters. On the defense perimeter the home forces were stationed in zones of defense, prepared to offer local resistance with air and naval support, while the reserves were moved. Churchill expected the army to concentrate twenty thousand men at any point within twelve hours.

The problem area ran from the Wash to Dover, for this was nearest to London. The sector from Dover to Land's End on the southwest coast was less menaced; there the air force and navy could keep track of shipping and make sure that no enemy warships could move across from the French Channel ports.

On the west coast the Germans would have to send large ships, and the Home Fleet and the air arm could be in action long before they reached a landing point. At this point, and particularly after the disruption of the French fleet in Africa, the Germans had no large ships available to escort landing forces. Thus it seemed impossible for the Germans to be so foolhardy as to send unarmed merchant ships into the teeth of a defense. But allowing for every assumption, the Admiralty was preparing to lay a minefield from Cornwall to Ireland, covering the Bristol Channel and the Irish Sea.

No area was left unwatched, even that bleak and lonely coast up by the Shetland and Faroes islands, which could be approached by the Germans only from Norway. Churchill and his generals distributed the home forces accordingly, covering every area in relation to the perceived need. While they were making these dispositions in mid-August, British intelligence did learn of the reality and the name of the German Operation Sea Lion, and that it was to be aimed at the south and west of England and not at the east as had seemed so obvious.

At the same time, the airmen and submariners were rewarded for their vigilance. A large number of self-propelled barges and motorboats began to pass along the French coast of the English Channel, through the Straits of Dover, and assemble at the French Channel ports from Calais to Brest. Aerial photographs showed the enemy progress day by day. Submarines and motor torpedo boats began to attack these vessels, and orders went out to Bomber Command to make daily raids on the ports.

The recovering British intelligence network also began to gather details about the forthcoming invasion attempt. Spies noted the movement of large numbers of troops by rail and truck, and concentrations in the Pas de Calais and Normandy areas. Even two mountain divisions were spotted with mules, apparently prepared to attack the Folkestone cliffs.

Because the British defense forces had planned an elastic defense, it was no trick, as Churchill said, "to shift our weight from one leg to the other and to improve all our facilities for moving our increasingly large mobile reserves towards the southern front," where the invasion threat seemed to be developing.

Meanwhile in August, the struggle for air superiority—"the Battle of Britain"—began. As the British defense chiefs knew very well, on the outcome of that battle would rest the fate of Hitler's invasion attempt.

By September the British had raised their force to a total of thirteen infantry divisions and three armored divisions on the south coast of Britain, in addition to the home defense forces which were the first line of defense. The sixteen divisions were the mobile reserve, prepared to move anywhere.

They were ever watchful. With the fall of France, the Germans had occupied the Channel Islands, so they were very close. Also all that concatenation of islands off the Belgian and Dutch coasts could conceal many thousands of troops, and from the disposition of the German forces, no one could tell when or where the attack would come.

The Admiralty made studies of weather and tides and concluded that the invasion attempt was most likely to occur between September 15 and September 30, and that it would probably come at dawn. The tension grew, but instead of being fearful, Churchill and the high command seemed to welcome the prospects, so confident were they of the British ability to first strike the enemy before he could land, and then to drive him back into the sea once he had committed his forces.

In July and August, Marshal Goering's Luftwaffe set out to make good on his boast that the German air force could win the war single-handedly. They did not. Perhaps they might have during one critical week when they had concentrated their air attacks on the British radar facilities and had put most of them out of action. At that time Britain's air defense hung by a slender thread, but Goering made the error of calling off the attacks as having done their job, and the British fighter command quickly recuperated. As it was with land invading forces, the attacker was at a disadvantage which only superior numbers could overcome. When the Germans came to fight over England, if they were shot down, they became prisoners of war, and were lost to the Luftwaffe, whereas the British could simply return to their bases and get another aircraft to fight again. By the end of August, the British had asserted air mastery of British skies, and particularly in the southeastern part of England, they were dominant.

The British coastline bristled with pillboxes, block houses, and defense systems. The Royal Navy was growing in strength, and its strength was concentrated on the defense of Britain, although it had to be at the expense of the convoys.

Among the Germans, the controversy about the breadth of the attack persisted until August 27, 1940, when Hitler issued a directive, which compromised the issue, to the satisfaction of neither army nor navy. The final plan called for Field Marshal von Rundstedt to land 113 divisions, with 12 in reserve. The Sixteenth Army was concentrated at ports between Rotterdam and Boulogne. It would land in the area of Hythe, Rye, Hastings, and Eastbourne. The Ninth Army, located at ports between Boulogne and Le Havre, would land between Brighton and Worthing. The forces would then swing around and capture Dover from the land, and then move toward Canterbury. Altogether the first wave would consist of eleven divisions. In a week the troops should be at Portsmouth. In reserve was the Sixth Army. And it would be very easy for the Germans to double their troop forces as they went along, because the whole European continent was quiet. Germany had triumphed, and she was unopposed in Europe.

By the beginning of September, the German navy reported to Hitler that it had 168 transports, 1,910 barges, 419 tugs and trawlers, and 1,600 motorboats available for the invasion. As these parts of the shipping picture were put together, they came under increasingly furious assault by the RAF, and by the Royal Navy. The German navy had provided a 10 percent margin for contingencies, and this had been exhausted, but the naval forces were still strong enough to do the job.

The German war machine was moving rapidly toward invasion day. On September 3 Field Marshal Keitel issued a new order:

"The earliest day for the sailing of the invasion fleet has been fixed as September 20, and that of the landing for September 21.

Order for the launching of the attack will be given D-minus-10 Day, presumably therefore on September 11.

Final commands will be given at the latest on D-minus-3 Day, at midday.

All preparations must remain liable to cancellation 24 hours before zero hour."

But Goering's promise could not be fulfilled; on August 30 the navy reported that because of the heavy British attacks on the shipping along the European coast, the navy could not be ready by September 15 for the assault. So the date was postponed until September 21. In addition, the navy had to have ten days warning, which meant the warning must be made by September 11.

In the first week of September, four German spies were put ashore on the southeast coast of England by submarine. But when they rowed in to shore in their rowboat, they were immediately captured by Home Guardsmen. When questioned, the four confessed their mission: to report on the movement of British reserves in the Ipswich-Oxford-London triangle. At almost the same time the British noted the increase of movement of small ships and barges to ports between Ostend and Le Havre, even though the ports were under constant air attack. This meant to the British that the invasion attempt was growing very close, otherwise the Germans would not risk their shipping thus.

Also the RAF noted that the strength of the Luftwaffe between Amsterdam and Brest had been increased by 160 bombers, which had been moved down from Norway, and that Stuka dive-bombers were being concentrated in the Pas de Calais region. On September 7, also, the Germans made their first big raid on London. It came about because earlier the British had conducted a small air raid against Berlin. Hitler had been furious. How dare the beaten British embarrass him so with the German people? He ordered Goering to retaliate. So on September 7, 1940, 625 German bombers, protected by 648 fighters, hit London, and by nightfall the docks were ablaze and the railroad lines to the south were completely blocked. All this gave the British home defense units the feeling that the invasion was imminent, and so that night the defense command put out the alert—"Cromwell" was the code word for the declaration that the invasion was imminent. The chiefs of staff did not believe this, really, but they had made no preparations for a "standby" situation. Therefore, the word was out that the Germans were coming.

The enthusiastic Home Guard had the word, as well as did the regulars. One unit of engineers blew up several key bridges lest they fall into the hands of the enemy. Thousands of Home Guardsmen responded with a will, setting church bells to ringing all over England to call out the guard. Rumors flew everywhere: The Germans had landed a parachute division. German E-boats were virtually up on the beach.

But it was all flummery, and the only ones really surprised were Prime Minister Churchill and the chiefs of staff, who had not been advised. Next morning all this was put to rights, and a system of "standby" was devised. As for the church bells, they were not to be rung unless the ringer personally saw at least twenty-five parachutists landing.

So the first crisis of the "invasion" had been overcome, and because of strict censorship, it did not make the newspapers, and was not mentioned in Parliament. But the preparations for the real invasion continued apace.

The bombing of Britain had passed into its third stage: first, the bombing of shipping and ports, then the attempt to knock out the RAF, and now the terror campaign levied against the civilian population in London and other cities.

In Germany, however, the enthusiasm for the invasion was decreasing rapidly. On September 6 Admiral Raeder had a long meeting with Hitler to discuss Operation Sea Lion. Actually, they talked about everything else but that. Raeder was eager to bring Hitler's mind to bear on other methods of winning the war with the British, and he talked about Norway, Gibraltar, the perfidious activities of the Americans in behalf of Britain, and the situation of the French colonies. (Japan was just then preparing to occupy French Indochina, with the assent of the Germans.) It was obvious at the end of that talk that Hitler was wavering, and Raeder was glad of it.

On September 10 Admiral Raeder's staff reported that the weather had turned on them and the British bombing had increased and they would not be ready. They could manage, but the most important qualification had not been met: the Luftwaffe had not achieved undisputed air superiority over the English Channel. Marshal Goering replied that his bombing of London was so effective that invasion might not be necessary after all. So on September 11 Hitler postponed the invasion again, for three days. It would be September 24.

On September 12 Naval Group West, the command in France, sent a worried message to Admiral Raeder, warning that interruptions of the invasion preparations by British air forces, long-range guns firing from the British coasts, and naval forces had for the first time put serious difficulties in the navy's way. The harbors at Ostend, Dunkirk, Calais, and Boulogne had to be evacuated at night because of British bombing and shelling. British warships roamed the Channel at will. All these developments were slowing the assembly of the invasion fleet.

On September 13 the news from Naval Group West was even more ominous. The British that day sank eighty barges in Ostend Harbor, and British warships bombarded all the ports mentioned, plus Cherbourg. On September 14 Admiral Raeder reassessed the whole plan. He noted that Marshal Goering had still not provided undisputed mastery of the air, and this meant the risk of failure of the whole operation was very great. If the British defeated the invasion attempt, Raeder observed, the psychological results in Europe would be severe. Now that the invasion was known to the British, it must be continued in the planning, to keep the British tension up. Cancellation would be a severe blow to the German

armed forces morale, and a big lift for the British. Therefore, the air attacks on Britain must continue at full
strength.

Hitler agreed. At a meeting of his senior military staff
that day, he indicated his impatience: the war was all but
won; he wanted to get the matter of Britain settled so he
could get on with his war in the East, his holy war against
devilish Bolshevism.

The best solution was still to invade Britain and get it
over with. She could not hope for help from Russia, and
the Americans would not be ready to fight until 1945 at
least. All that was needed now was about a week of good
weather and the Luftwaffe would have Britain defeated,
he was sure. But Hitler admitted that it was very troublesome to have the British keep picking themselves up
off the floor, and that enemy fighter planes had still not
been eliminated as a factor in the air. So they must wait
a little longer.

Raeder was temporizing. As far as the navy was concerned, matters were going from bad to worse. On September 14, in Antwerp Harbor, five transports were badly
damaged by air attack, one barge was sunk, and two
loading cranes were destroyed. An ammunition train was
blown up, and several warehouses went up, too.

On September 17 there was a full moon over the English Channel, and that night the British night bombers
sank eighty-four barges at Dunkirk, and blew up a five-
hundred-ton ammunition depot at Cherbourg. Along the
coast, other installations were destroyed: a ration depot,
half a dozen steamships, several torpedo boats. It was
necessary to disperse the ships from the harbors across
from the English shore guns, and to stop further movement of ships into the invasion ports.

And so that night it became apparent that the invasion
would have to be suspended for a long while. It was seen
that the British were totally aware of the plan, and were
taking many countermeasures, and that the countermea-

sures of the RAF and the British fleet were effective already. Raeder also knew that the Home Fleet was poised, and ready to do battle. More than thirty British destroyers had been located by German air reconnaissance in the southern waters of Britain, which meant that the British were preoccupied with the invasion in the area that it was supposed to occur.

And above all, the Luftwaffe had failed to perform. So after five uninterrupted years of military successes, Adolf Hitler had finally been stopped. On September 19 he ordered the cessation of the assembly of shipping, to reduce losses. The charade continued until October 12, when Hitler finally issued a directive calling off the operation indefinitely, although apparent preparations would continue to keep pressure on Britain. The bombing of Britain was to continue, and some other method must be found to defeat the British. But now, for the first time, Hitler realized that it was going to be a long, hard war.

CHAPTER 9

Britain Strikes Back

One of the major reasons that the Germans called off their invasion of Britain in the fall of 1940 was their failure to conquer the Royal Air Force in the Battle of Britain. But an almost equally powerful reason was the unexpectedly effective resistance of the British home defenses.

Just after the collapse of the British Expeditionary Force at Dunkirk, Prime Minister Churchill had ordered the arming of Dover promontory and other coastal highlands with guns capable of shooting across the English Channel.

At Dover the British put up a fourteen-inch gun, and by September it was engaging in duels with the German shore batteries on the other side of the Channel that were firing on British convoys. Two 13.5-inch railway guns were also put into action, moving along the coastline. They had been taken from the old battleship *Iron Duke*. Naval Group West complained to Berlin that the British defenses onshore and the British forays by submarine, destroyer, and motor torpedo boat were making it impossible to assemble the invasion flotilla. That argument was a big factor in Admiral Raeder's resistance to the invasion attempt, and ultimately a factor in Hitler's decision to postpone the invasion indefinitely.

Another factor in the postponement was the failure of German intelligence to secure accurate information about

British home defenses. And the story of this failure is very much the story of MI5, the British counterintelligence agency that was so effective, the Germans had not managed to put an intelligence system into place in Britain during the prewar years. Although there were few restrictions on travel and immigration in those years, the British had developed a simple means of control of foreigners coming into the country.

At the end of World War I, Britain had enacted an Aliens Registration Act, which gave immigration officers control over the entry of any foreigner. This was arbitrary, but denial of landing permits was seldom invoked, and only against known troublemakers or criminals. But, more important, the law provided that the alien must register with the police, and keep them informed of his movements. Thus, through the police, the government could keep control of all aliens in the country.

When the war began in September 1939, 71,600 aliens were registered with the British police. Of these, 400 were on a list of people whom MI5 considered too dangerous to remain at liberty. These represented the German intelligence system's attempts to infiltrate and set up an espionage system. Most of these people were German nationals who had been working in Britain. Some of them were employed as domestic servants in the households of military personnel. About thirty-five, who held British nationality, were sent to Brixton prison under provisions of the Defence of the Realm Act. Immediately on the outbreak of war, all the German and Austrian nationals in Britain were ordered up for questioning and processing by 120 Kings's Counsel and county judges. All of them were first sent to internment camp reception centers while they waited for this processing. Thus MI5 rounded up the *Abwehr* (German intelligence agents), without their knowing they were even especially suspected.

Concentration camps were set up on the Isle of Man

and in Lancashire. Some internees were sent to Canada, including one shipload aboard the steamer *Arandora Star*, which was sunk in mid-Atlantic in July 1940 by Lieutenant Commander Guenther Prien in *U–47*, with heavy loss of life, most of them German internees.

Some, who were regarded as suspect but about whom there was question, had been granted limited freedom. The vast majority, about fifty-two thousand people, had been judged to be "refugees from Nazi oppression."

But even before Dunkirk, after the Germans broke through the Meuse line, attitudes in Britain changed. Suspicion was the order of the day. "We cannot be too sure of anybody," said Field Marshal Sir Redmond Ironside, commander of British Home Forces. MI5 had long lists of Nazi sypathizers, and others who felt that the dangers of Bolshevism were so great that Nazism was to be welcomed. In February 1940 a "New British Broadcasting Station" had started beaming programs from Germany to Britain, to create confusion and dissension. One of its primary themes was that Churchill was a warmonger, and by summer the station was talking about the "imminent invasion of Britain."

No one knew how many people listened to such broadcasts as those of the Christian Peace Movement, operating from Hamburg, but the authorities were, by the summer of 1940, becoming very sensitive to constant public complaint about a Fifth Column. William Saxton-Steer, a member of Sir Oswald Moseley's British Union of Fascists, was caught sticking an advertisement for the New British Broadcasting Service on the glass wall of a telephone kiosk. So great was the public outrage that he was sentenced to seven years for treason.

The broadcasts continued, emphasizing the growing strength of the Fifth Column and continuing to claim that invasion was imminent. The newspapers were full of stories about the Nazi Fifth Columns in France, Belgium, and Holland. A sort of "spy mania" gripped the British people, and in this fright, the government declared a coastal belt from Inverness, Scotland, to Dorset, to be a special protected zone. All Austrian and German males between sixteen and sixty were interned. All the internees were examined.

So numerous were the reports of sabotage and Fifth Column activity that a special Invasion Warning Sub-committee was appointed in the Admiralty. On the day they first met, they considered a telephone report by Admiral Sir Bertram Ramsay, the commander at Dover, that many acts of sabotage and Fifth Column work had been found at Dover. That same day, May 31, 1940, an order went out from the government calling for the re-moval of all road signposts and place names throughout the country. This was done to confuse German parachu-tists, who were expected to land momentarily. What it did was thoroughly confuse the British people traveling in strange areas, and foreign allies who did not know the countryside. A popular explanation for the speed of the German conquest of Belgium, Holland, and France was that the Fifth Column had effectively sabotaged defenses in all these countries.

The British home defenders vowed that this would never happen in Britain. So nine hundred beaches on the south coast of England were booby-trapped, and Major General Colin McV. Gubbins, commander of the Home Guard, vowed to fight the Germans on the beaches. Plans were made to move the Cabinet War Room from beneath Great George Street to the Post Office Research Station at Dollis Hill. The Admiralty, and the War Office and other vital units, were all to move. But the plans were scotched by Prime Minister Churchill, who foresaw noth-ing but confusion in them. The whole idea collapsed on September 20, 1940, when the place where the cabinet was supposed to be meeting was bombed by the Ger-mans.

The newspapers were not much help, either. One paper

printed a story of the forging of Bank of England notes in the millions of pounds, and thousands in Britain began to distrust their own money. Another paper declared that foot-and-mouth disease had broken out in England and that British meat was contaminated. Another said sabotage was crippling British industry.

The newspapers continued to complain, and not just the newspapers. The Registrar of Oxford University complained that there were more than 1,000 foreigners in Oxford, 477 of them enemy aliens. "Aliens are a potential menace, and we feel they should be interned," he told a reporter from the *Times*. "They can be sorted out after internment if necessary."

Hundreds of complaints deluged the MI5 office at Wormwood Scrubs about Fifth Column activity. One agent was assigned to inspect all the telephone poles in the southern counties and submit a security report on each one. Someone had charged that Fifth Columnists were leaving messages on telephone poles for the German parachutists.

"Loose talk sinks ships," said the BBC and the posters all over the country. William Jackson, an airfield laborer, was talking in a pub one night about his job, and some airmen heard him mention that he worked at the airfield. He was convicted and sent to prison for a month. One day in June a mother and daughter on the banks of the Tyne were heard to comment about the passing ships. They were denounced by a group of schoolboys and fined five pounds each. An airwoman was heard by a busman in a pub to commend Hitler. "Hitler has wonderful organization. It is the very thing we need in this country— someone with dictatorial powers." She was convicted and went to prison for three months for starting rumors.

Thousands more people were sent to camps, and by the end of June 1940, Major General Sir Vernon Kell, director of MI5, felt confident that all the spies in Britain had been rounded up. Further, he had a way of checking up—a double agent with the code name SNOW.

In the middle of May 1940, MI5 scored a victory. An agent named Joan Miller had been assigned to infiltrate the Right Club, an organization founded by Captain Archibald H. M. Ramsay, a Unionist member of Parliament. He was a member of the Anglo-German Fellowship and very pro-Hitler. One of his associates was Anna Wolkoff, an anti-Semite and anti-Communist. She and her father and mother (he was a White Russian admiral) opened a tearoom opposite the South Kensington tube station, which soon became a center of right-wing activity.

Miss Miller's job was to get a list of the membership of the Right Club, so all could be scooped up when wanted. In the course of infiltrating, she was told by Miss Wolkoff that the club would welcome any information Miss Miller could bring from her "dull filing job at the War Office." So MI5 turned its special attention to Miss Wolkoff and discovered that she was holding secret meetings with Colonel Francesco Maringliano, assistant naval attaché at the Italian Embassy, and was also intimate with a cipher clerk from the American Embassy, Tyler Kent. It became apparent that the Italian Embassy was using Miss Wolkoff as a pipeline into the American Embassy. This all tied up with reports that the German ambassador to Rome had access to Prime Minister Winston Churchill's secret correspondence with President Franklin D. Roosevelt. The indications were strong enough that they were taken to American Ambassador Joseph Kennedy, and he agreed to waive Tyler Kent's diplomatic immunity. On May 20 Kent's flat in Gloucester Place was raided by the police, who found there fifteen hundred classified documents from the American Embassy. Kent admitted to taking documents since the fall of 1939 and showing them to Captain Ramsay. There was the connection between the British Fifth Column and the Germans.

Later in the year, Kent and Miss Wolkoff were tried and found guilty under the Official Secrets Act. He was sent to prison for seven years. Miss Wolkoff was convicted of taking documents from Kent and of having sent a coded letter to Lord Haw Haw, the German propagandist in Berlin. Lord Haw Haw's real name was William Joyce, and he had gone to live in Berlin in August 1939 and begun broadcasting for the Germans in September. He was a close associate of Captain Ramsay. On the basis of the convictions and suspicions, Captain Ramsay was arrested, in spite of his "Parliamentary privilege," and held in prison until 1944.

The British defense authorities became seriously worried on May 26, 1940, when the chiefs of staff were informed that the crushing defeat in France had resulted in the complete disruption of the Secret Intelligence Services, and that, therefore, the government could not expect any previous warning from sources on the continent regarding German plans for invasion. The only reliable information would have to come from aerial reconnaissance.

All that summer the worry continued. The first invasion alarm came early in August, when the Foreign Office suggested that information obtained from neutral sources indicated attack was imminent. On July 29 cipher intercepts had indicated something, too: for the first time, the Luftwaffe had been ordered to refrain from bombing ports in the south of England. Just such an order had been imposed by the Luftwaffe just before the assault on France began. So the conclusion was not hard to draw: the Germans wanted to save the ports for their invasion forces.

Then, in mid-August, came another flare.

On August 12 a message from a *Fliegerkorps* commander demanded the transfer of thirty men with perfect command of English to his command. On the morning of August 14, Home Guardsmen found some eighty parachutes scattered around the Midlands, and a great deal of paraphernalia suitable for sabotage, plus maps, saddlebags, wireless sets, and lists of targets. That morning the Home Guard began a major chase of the invaders, but not a single parachutist was found. Eventually it was established that the "drop" had been a propaganda ploy.

The second parachute scare came in early September, to a nervous English defense organization. For weeks the RAF Photo Reconnaissance unit had noticed a buildup of landing craft and activity at several ports on the English Channel, particularly Ostend and Calais, which housed hundreds of landing barges. On the morning of September 3, three *Abwehr* agents were captured in Kent, and a fourth was soon picked up. They confirmed their status: they were the advance guard for the invasion, which could be expected at any moment. Their assigned task had been to radio reports on the state of the British defenses. Then came announcement that the Wehrmacht had canceled all leave on September 8. And the meteorologists said that the tide and weather conditions for September 9 and 10 were ideal for invasion. All that was what had prompted the flash of the code word CROMWELL, and the hunt for invaders on the night of September 7.

In the fall of 1940, the British had the Italians confused and the Germans flummoxed. Count Ciano, the Italian foreign minister, stated the case in a puzzled note in his diary on September 11, 1940. "It seems incredible, but we do not have a single informant in Great Britain. On the other hand, the Germans have many. In London itself there is a German agent who makes radio transmissions up to twenty-nine times a day. At least so it is stated by Admiral Canaris [chief of the German *Abwehr* intelligence agency]."

Count Ciano's puzzlement would have changed to amusement had he known the truth about the many agents the Germans claimed to have in Britain. For without exception, at this time they were plants, "double agents" who were feeding the Germans just what the British wanted them to know.

This provision of information was more difficult than it might seem, because the Germans were not fools. Therefore, at least some of the information they received had to be highly secret, accurate, and at least apparently valuable to the Germans. That was the rub; how could British counterintelligence supply the enemy with information without hurting the war effort?

In July 1940, when intelligence became a critical factor in the war, MI5 created a special wireless board which vetted the material sent to the Germans by the double agents.

The whole system of double agents started with Arthur George Owens, a Welshman born in 1899, who had before the war emigrated to Canada. In 1933 Owens returned to Britain and formed a company that built storage batteries and sold them to the Royal Navy, among other clients. Through the naval connection, Owens was persuaded to work for British Naval Intelligence. He made several visits to German shipyards before the war, and reported as an enthusiastic volunteer to Naval Intelligence on his findings. It was a great shock, then, to Naval Intelligence to learn one day in 1936 that Owens was in communication with a known *Abwehr* cover address in Germany—P.O. Box 6629, Hamburg. The British, of course, opened all outgoing mail addressed to that box, and thus learned that Owens was trying to arrange a meeting with *Abwehr* agents in Cologne. This fact was discovered by SIS, Secret Intelligence Service, a part of MI6, and the control officers decided to let Owens keep the appointment and see what happened. When he returned, he went to SIS with the story voluntarily: the Germans had asked him to work for *Abwehr*. MI6 did not like the idea, so they turned him over to MI5, and for three years Owens kept up his relationship with the Germans, under MI5 supervision.

In January 1939 the Germans sent him a wireless set, which he turned over to the police. The result was embarrassing in a peculiarly British sort of way. Having taken the set apart, the police were unable to get it back together again. A very embarrassing bumble, which did not help Owens's confidence in MI5.

In August, Owens moved out on his wife and house and moved in with a woman named Mrs. Funnell, of German extraction. He took her to Germany for two weeks. When he returned, he disappeared. But he surfaced on September 4, the day after war was declared. He was jailed at Wandsworth prison under the war laws, but he soon became a real double agent, and MI5 learned that he had a whole network of *Abwehr* agents. On September 28 Owens, who now had the British code name SNOW, went to Holland, and then to Antwerp, where he met with three members of the *Abwehr* for an afternoon. Soon Owens and his "chief agent" were in Belgium again. The chief agent was a retired Welsh policeman named Gwilym Williams. He posed as a Welsh nationalist who was willing to run sabotage operations for the Germans.

By the end of 1939 the "Welsh ring" established by the *Abwehr* was functioning, but not as the Germans thought. Owens was in almost daily communication with Germany, giving a mixture of true and false information. Williams was busily planning Plan Guy Fawkes, a scheme to poison the water reservoirs in Wales. Through contacts with Owens, several other agents were also recruited as double agents. Ultimately the network numbered fourteen people. Soon enough, Owens was found not to be a double agent but a triple agent. He had started for the Germans, gone over to the British to dupe the Germans, but then told the Germans he was a double agent and had agreed to *really* work for them. Owens then came under careful surveillance.

The Germans kept trying to get their intelligence organization going. They sent three South Africans to Ireland, where they were promptly arrested in July 1940. They tried to work through the Spanish Embassy, but MI5 penetrated the Spanish Embassy.

Between April and September of 1940, six *Abwehr* spies were intercepted by the Irish. More were intercepted in Britain. The Germans kept trying valiantly, and the British kept fending them off. As a result, by the fall of 1940, the intelligence the Germans were getting about affairs in Britain was all carefully manufactured.

One by one, agents were dropped by parachute into Britain, where they were usually swiftly spotted and then arrested. Gosta Caroli, a Swede, was arrested when he landed in Northampton, and made another of MI5's double agents. On September 19 Wyulf Schmidt was dropped by a black Heinkel bomber in Cambridgeshire, and promptly arrested. Hans Reysen landed in Northamptonshire, and after four days was arrested. They all were supposed to report on the morale and defenses of England, and they did, but not quite the way the Germans had expected. After being recruited by MI5, these double agents traveled back and forth to the continent, often to Lisbon, where the *Abwehr* had an important post. They went with vetted information and returned with money and supplies for their work. The Germans really believed they had a functioning intelligence organization in England. But the agents who actually came in were either promptly arrested and turned, or were jailed, tried, and executed. Sixteen German agents were executed in Britain during the war. Only one man was known to have spied for the Germans in Britain during the war and not apprehended. He was Jan Willen Ter Brak, who had turned up in Cambridge in 1940 claiming to be a Dutch refugee. Papers indicated that he had moved around among the various airfields, and it had to be presumed that he sent some information back to the Germans. But it did not last long. He was found dead, a suicide in an air raid shelter in Cambridge on April Fool's Day 1941.

In all, the most successful agent the Germans had in Britain was the Welshman Owens, named No. 3504 by the *Abwehr*. His signal accomplishment could have been fatal to the British defense effort. It was made on September 18, 1939, and was entitled "personal observations and from the Dutch War Ministry engineer with Phillips in England." The report concerned a net of ultra-high-frequency stations to monitor enemy aircraft approaching along the British coast from the Isle of Wight to the Orkneys. He further reported that the device made it possible to estimate the distance of the aircraft and the number of engines. It had three stages: Advance, Intermediate, and Final. It was operating from stations in Suffolk, Essex, and Kent counties. It could be identified by the tall wooden or steel towers 250–350 feet high. When Admiral Canaris, the chief of the German *Abwehr*, saw the report, he said, "This may yet turn out to be the most important piece of intelligence we'll ever get."

He was right. The Germans had discovered the British radar.

CHAPTER 10

Britain at Bay

In the late spring of 1940 the beleaguered British had to revise their war production schedules and do all possible to produce the materials of war to replace the enormous losses in France. Take tanks, for example. After Dunkirk, there was scarcely a tank in Britain, and in the old days it had taken nearly a year to produce one. But Churchill discovered that the Germans could produce a tank in nine months, and so he knew that the British could do the same.

Churchill was constantly pressing his associates for action. He wanted a thousand tanks produced in the next few months. He kept after Professor Frederick Lindemann, his scientific adviser, for news about the proximity fuse for antiaircraft guns, a fuse that would work in the same way as the acoustic torpedo in the sea, exploding in the vicinity of a target. The problem here was that the government had to let an experimental contract for development. Churchill said they let two or three such contracts, by competition to speed the process.

Even though the British army had been decimated in France, under Churchill's insistent gaze, it began reviving. By mid-July Churchill was talking about a whole series of raids to be conducted against the Germans on the continent.

Sir Roger Keyes was making a special study for Churchill of these raids, to use not less than ten thousand men, nor more than five thousand. Churchill hoped to carry out two or three such raids in the course of the coming winter. They were specifically designed to tie up large numbers of German troops in France and Norway. And looking ahead, Churchill was planning for larger and stronger forays against the French coast in the following year. As if the war with Germany were not enough, Churchill and his cabinet had now to deal with the restless movement of Japan, whose government was still hoping to force the capitulation of Chiang Kai-shek's Nationalist forces. In July the British had been blackmailed into closing the Burma Road, because they did not have the resources to face up to Japan at the moment. Churchill was under no illusions, however, about the Japanese. In August he was planning for the day that the Japanese would declare war, which he fully expected. In Japan then a furious debate was raging over the proposed alliance that the army wanted to sign with Germany and Italy. The navy, by and large, opposed the move, but the army was strengthening its control of the government, and the navy was fighting a losing battle, as could be clearly seen from London. If war came, what would be the Admiralty's plan? Churchill inquired. And he demanded full details on the new Japanese battleships, the *Yamato* and the *Musashi*, which were joining the Japanese fleet.

By the end of the year 1940, the Australians were calling for the strengthening of Singapore, but Britain was in no position to do much about it, as Churchill wrote to Prime Minister Robert Menzies of Australia. The Australians offered to send troops, but they wanted Britain to increase the naval defenses of the base.

Churchill did not agree that the Japanese menace was growing worse. He felt that there was less danger at the end of 1940 than there had been six months earlier just after the fall of France.

One reason for the survival of Britain in that summer

of 1940, when she stood alone against the Germans, can be found in the story of an obscure scientific officer who in 1939 held a minor post on the staff of the British Ministry in London. He was R. V. Jones, and his work involved the whole story of the British scientific world, the impact of its work on the war effort.

Early in June 1940, The RAF became aware through code interception and breach of the Enigma machine code of the Germans that the enemy had some sort of radio beam to bring them into England. Professor Lindemann, scientific adviser to Prime Minister Churchill, called in R. V. Jones for information. Jones was sure that the Germans had a sort of radar operating, an intersecting beam system for the bombing of England. He investigated the bombers available to the Germans and found that the Heinkel III would be the craft involved. What he needed to know was what sort of equipment would be fitted to the aircraft to receive the beam. By RAF questioning of captive air crews, eventually he got the answer when one prisoner said to another that the British would never find the equipment. So far so good, for he then knew that the equipment did exist and was harnessed to the aircraft. It was simply a question of finding the treasure under their noses. Finally he found it in a receiver installed ostensibly for the purpose of blind landing. But this receiver was so much more sensitive than the need that he recognized it for what it was: the sensor for the beam to lead the German bombers to England. The device had been developed at Rechlin. It involved two intersecting radio beams. Soon the British had a prisoner from the Luftwaffe who said he was against the war, and agreed to cooperate. He drew a sketch of one of the transmitting towers. Jones recalled seeing photos of such a tower located near Hoernum on the island of Sylt, in Schleswig-Holstein, near the Danish border.

On June 14 Churchill appointed Air Marshal Sir Philip Joubert to be officer in charge of solving the problem of the beams. Next Joubert held a meeting with Jones and Lindemann and his staff, and it was decided that action should be taken.

What action?

First, they would jam the radio signals with nonsense racket. Second, they would search for concealed radios in Britain that might be involved in the homing system. Each week a report would be made to Churchill. Professor Lindemann set out to create new receivers capable of detecting the transmissions.

There was an air of urgency about this problem. On June 16 the British RAF staff estimated that the threat of invasion was imminent—possible within the week, likely within two weeks, and probable within three weeks.

The scientists selected five of the radar stations in Britain's coastal chain to try to detect these beams, and a special unit of the RAF.

The detection effort began on June 18. From an aircraft shot down in France before the Dunkirk evacuation, they were able to locate the two transmitting towers. The matter was so important in Churchill's view that Jones was summoned on June 20 to a meeting of the special defense committee at the prime minister's house, No. 10 Downing Street. Churchill presided and listened to Dr. Jones for twenty minutes without interrupting. It was then agreed that planes would be sent to try to discover the beams.

Churchill believed, but the RAF did not. That same day, with a flight scheduled for the night, they tried to scrub the entire project. Only when Dr. Jones threatened to tell Churchill did they back down. The flights were made, and the pilots reported that they discovered the beams.

What Churchill soon learned was that the Germans believed this beam weapon to be a decisive factor in their bombing of Britain. Whereas the British trained their air crews in the arts of navigation, the Germans did not. Why should they? They had the beams, and the beams could be focused on any target. All the pilot had to do was follow his beams and drop his bombs, and then follow his beams back home. It seemed ultimately simple.

But the British had a few ideas about that, too.

On August 23 the Knickebein beam stations near Dieppe and Cherbourg were trained on the big industrial complex of Birmingham. The Germans had settled on a large-scale night offensive to flatten Birmingham. But the British had learned how to jam the beams, and they did. They also deflected the beams and made them worse than useless, because by following the deflected beam, the German air crews got completely lost. Churchill later related one story that illustrates how effective the bending of the beams was: One of his subordinates sent his wife and children to the country so they would not be in danger in London as the air raids grew worse. They lived in a house ten miles away from the nearest town. One night they were astounded to see a series of explosions of heavy bombs in bare fields. They counted a hundred bombs exploding thus. The officer came back to the Churchill circle with this odd story, and sought an explanation. He did not get it. So tight was the security about the bending of the beams that not even an intimate of the prime minister could be told unless there was need for him to know.

The reason for the intense secrecy was legitimate enough, for had it been known, say, to Parliament, then the secret most certainly would have gotten out and filtered its way through the neutral countries to Germany. As it was, Goering said with great satisfaction that the beam system was infallible and threatened with the direst punishments any who gainsaid him. So for two months the Germans bombed and bombed, using their Knickebein stations, and by British estimate, four-fifths of their bombs fell outside the target areas, many of them into barren fields. The Wizard War had brought Britain its first big success, although as Churchill said, even a fifth of the bombs that the Germans dropped was enough to make the British very uncomfortable.

After two months, the Germans finally got onto the fact that the Knickebein beam was not working. They did, however, have another beam system used by one group, Kampf Gruppe 100, and this had not been diverted by the British. They were working on a jamming system, but it was not yet perfected, when the German air high command suddenly erupted in activity to recoup. The Gruppe 100 then became a Pathfinder group. On a raid, the Gruppe 100 planes would go in first, carrying incendiaries, and the fires they started in the target area would then become beacons for the rest of the Luftwaffe air strike of the night.

So in the autumn the German bombing became more accurate and more deadly.

By this time the Germans had switched their strategy. In that night raid of August 23, the German bombardiers had erred in the bombing runs, and instead of dropping their high-explosives on the target of the night, oil storage facilities and aircraft factories in South London, they had bombed north of the Thames, plastering a residential area and killing a number of civilians. The RAF believed this to be purposeful, and so the next night staged their first air raid on Berlin. It was a bad night—Berlin was hidden by a dense cover of low-lying clouds—and only half of the eighty-one British bombers actually found the target. They were subjected to intensive antiaircraft fire from two rings of antiaircraft artillery that surrounded the city, and searchlights penciled among the clouds, occasionally shifting fast to try to follow a target. The antiaircraft fire, although intense, was inaccurate, and no British bombers were brought down, but the damage they did was minor, too. Still, as radio correspondent William L. Shirer, who was there, noted the next day, the raid was an enormous shock to the German people, because Goering had been saying they need not worry about bombing from the Allies because Berlin was impregnable. In the morning, flying squads of police rushed around the city picking up leaflets dropped by the British, but the citizenry found enough of them to learn that the British promised to continue bombing Berlin as long as the war lasted, and that the war would last as long as Hitler did.

The RAF returned, as promised, on the night of August 28, and this time killed ten people and wounded twenty-eight.

COWARDLY BRITISH ATTACK

shrieked the German press the next day, on orders from Dr. Goebbels, who had suppressed the news of the first attack, but now in a change of Nazi policy accused the British of making war on defenseless women and children.

Two nights later, the RAF was back over Berlin for a third time, and the next day the headlines shrieked again

BRITISH AIR PIRATES OVER BERLIN!

The bombings were not very accurate and not very deadly, but after a week of them, the people of Berlin were already weary and disillusioned with their leaders' promises. Further, they were confused, because they could not understand what was happening. Germany had won victory after victory and now controlled most of the European continent. She had no open enemies except the one across the English Channel. And yet with all these victories, she did not have the peace for which most Germans yearned. The fact became paramount on September 1, the anniversary of the attack on Poland. On

September 4 Hitler used the opening of the Winterhilfe campaign as an excuse for a major policy address. He ridiculed Churchill and the British leaders, and he promised that England would be invaded. That was a vague remark, but it was believed. More important was what he had to say about the bombings, which was duly noted in London. The British were dropping three or four thousand kilograms of bombs on Berlin, he said. Let them wait. Soon the Germans would be dropping 300,000 or 400,000 kilograms of bombs each night on London. His listeners, mostly nurses and social workers, applauded hysterically as Hitler promised to raze the British cities.

And so, on the heels of wildly popular approval, even as the Luftwaffe admitted that it had not destroyed the British air force or its will to fight, Hitler approved a basic change of air strategy. On the brink of success, the daylight air attacks on the fighter installations were halted, and the massive night bombing of British cities, called "the Blitz," began.

When Count Ciano, the Italian foreign minister, heard the recording of Hitler's Winterhilfe speech, he observed that "Hitler must be growing nervous." There was good reason. Hitler knew by this time that the invasion of Britain would have to be called off. He knew also that the German people were clamoring for the end of the war. He was flabbergasted that the British continued to fight, and he did not know what to do. Admiral Raeder was after him to move the scene of military operations to the Mediterranean, and strike at Britain's empire, but Hitler continued to believe that if he could bring down the British government, then he could deal with the British people. Not all of them, he reasoned, could be as obdurate as Churchill. So Hitler allowed himself to be persuaded once more by Hermann Goering, who claimed that he could, indeed, raze Britain's cities and bring the British to terms by massive bombing.

As noted, late on the afternoon of September 7, 1940,

the change of strategy began. That day the Germans sent over London 625 bombers and 648 fighters. They flew up the Thames and concentrated on the Woolwich arsenal and the London docks. Before darkness fell, the dock area was a sea of flames. When this wave of bombers left, another raid of 250 bombers came in, and then another, and another, so that all night long the Germans attacked London, stopping only at dawn. The next night, Sunday, the Germans were back. At the end of two nights, more than eight hundred Londoners had been killed and nearly twenty-five hundred wounded.

All that next week the assault continued; every night the bombers came. And on September 15 it was to be climaxed by a great daylight raid.

In this first part of September, with the pressure off the fighter airfields, British Fighter Command swiftly rebuilt its strength, and on September 15 was ready for the daylight assault. The Germans sent two hundred bombers and six hundred fighters on this raid. The radar was working again, and long before the Germans arrived, the fighter fields were ready for them. The pilots waited and then manned their planes and intercepted the Germans before they reached London. Most of the formation was dispersed and many German planes were shot down before they reached the outskirts of London. Two hours later another German formation came, and was also turned back with minimal damage.

Too late, Goering's air commanders learned that they had not, as they had believed, wiped out the British fighter force, but instead they faced a force so strong that they could not carry out a successful daylight air raid on London. Two days later the invasion of Britain, Operation Sea Lion, was officially abandoned.

Instead, Britain was to be treated to a dose of terror. Hitler had opted for himself the decisions about terror raids on the enemy, and now he ordered Goering to raze the British cities. For the next fifty-seven nights the Ger-

mans would do their best, hitting London so hard that
secretly Churchill wondered if it would not become one
huge pile of rubble. London was not alone. Coventry
and other cities would feel the brutal might of the German
bombings that autumn of 1940 as Goering tried to do
what Hitler had been unable to do, knock Britain out of
the war.

The Germans continued to work on the directional
homing beams, and the British continued to work to
circumvent them. The British mastered the new X beam,
but then the Germans came up with a Y beam. But the
British scientists were quicker than the Germans, and
they were ready to make it useless by the time it became
operational. On the first night of its use, the British were
ready, and their countermethod threw the Germans off.
The German air crews could be heard muttering on the
radio; they never developed any faith in this weapon after
that first night of failure. They were so far thrown off
the track that one night they bombed Dublin in neutral
Eire by mistake, much to the chagrin of the German high
command.

In 1940 the British were working hard to improve their
radar operations on the sea and in the air. They had
quickly developed an air system called A.I., which had
been under research since 1938. By 1940 it was crude
but fairly effective. The system was too cumbersome for
a pilot to operate, so it was installed in two-seater Blenheim bombers, and later in Beaufighters, in which the
second man was the radar operator, who directed the
pilot until he could close with the enemy and attack with
visual observation. With the application of this system,
the German beams became an asset for the British, because by finding the beam, the night fighters knew when
and where the German attack was going to be directed.
The German bomber losses rose steadily, until finally in
the spring of 1941, they broke off the night attacks and
gave up the attempt to bomb Britain into submission. By

that time the Germans were deeply involved in the Mediterranean and were about to plunge into the mire of the Russian campaign.

Meanwhile the British scientists were working on other devices. Radar, of course, was recognized as an invaluable system for antiaircraft defense, and the British antiaircraft gunners were being trained to use it. The improvement in radar would be continual, the Allies would always be far ahead of their enemies in this field, and it would be a major factor in the Allied victory both in the European theater and in the Pacific.

CHAPTER 11

The German Dilemma

In the autumn of 1940, having conquered Czechoslovakia and Poland, allied himself with the Soviets to protect his eastern border, and conquered Holland and Belgium and France, Hitler was still uneasy. There was no peace, and Britain vowed that there would be no peace until the Third Reich was destroyed.

Hitler and his generals were preoccupied with Britain; only Grand Admiral Erich Raeder kept counseling that attention should now be turned to the Mediterranean, and the British presence there destroyed. In the summer, after the French situation had been resolved, Field Marshal Keitel went on leave. When he returned to Berchtesgaden on August 10, Keitel had no idea what Hitler wanted next. But from his own observation, he knew that there was now no hope of a quick end to the war with Britain. Why? Because he sensed that the United States had already cast her lot with Britain and that "all her unlimited resources" stood behind Britain. This was a shrewd impression, not publicly supported, and it must have come from the secret correspondence between President Franklin D. Roosevelt and Prime Minister Churchill, to which the Germans had access through the espionage of the Italians, who, as noted, had a pipeline in code clerk Tyler Kent in the American Embassy in London.

On July 23 a British trade commission in America reached agreement with the U.S. government, permitting the British to buy 40 percent of the American aircraft production. On July 24, 1940, Roosevelt, Secretary of the Navy Frank Knox, and Churchill agreed that the United States would give the British fifty badly needed old coal-burning destroyers for antisubmarine work in exchange for leases on British territory in the western hemisphere, which would be used to build American naval bases. That agreement had not been announced and would not be for a month, but it was the first major commitment of the United States government to Britain in its hour of need, and Field Marshal Keitel was quite right in considering it a major step in American policy.

The German Empire itself was quiet enough. Even before Hitler had invaded Poland, he had known what he was going to do with the Polish people: they were to be made into a nation of slaves. At the conference with the generals in Obersalzburg just before the attack, Hitler had warned the generals that they would not like some of the things that were going to happen in Poland but that they were not to interfere with the Nazis, but instead to stick to their military duties. In conversation with one of his generals, Hitler had laid it out, and after the talk, the shocked general remembered:

"We have no intention of rebuilding Poland. Polish intelligentsia must be prevented from establishing itself as a governing class. Low standard of living must be conserved. Cheap slaves. Total disorganization must be created. The Reich will give the governor general the means to carry out this devilish plan."

The Nazi atrocities began during the campaign. On September 10 the troops of a Nazi artillery regiment beat up fifty Jews all day, then herded them into a synagogue and massacred them. They were caught, captured, tried, and sentenced: to one year in prison. General Georg von Keuchler, commander of the Third Army, rejected the sentences as too light. But Hitler meant what he had told his generals: don't interfere. Heinrich Himmler, chief of the SS, went to Army Commander in Chief von Brauchitsch, who overruled the general and quashed the sentences altogether.

The army did its best to keep its own skirts clear. General Halder knew that the Nazis intended to exterminate the nobility and the Polish clergy and the Jews. But the army insisted that this extermination plan be deferred until Poland was turned over to civil administration, and Himmler had to agree.

In October 1939 Poland had been partitioned, and the old German provinces became part of the Third Reich. Russia had taken her territory in the East. What was left was designated by Hitler as the General Government of Poland, and the Nazi Hans Frank was appointed governor, with the Austrian Nazi Arthur Seyss-Inquart as his deputy.

"The Poles," said Governor Frank, "shall be the slaves of the German Reich."

Himmler and his deputy Reinhard Heydrich were given responsibility for liquidating the Polish Jews. Frank and Seyss-Inquart were to liquidate the intelligentsia, the nobility, and the clergy.

In the fall of 1939, the movement of populations began. The Germans from the Baltic were moved into the annexed Polish provinces, and the Poles were moved out into the territory of the General Government. Before the fall of 1940, 1.2 million Poles and three hundred thousand Jews had been moved into that holocaust area. In June the Germans opened a new prison camp at Auschwitz. It was created for the harsh treatment of Polish political prisoners, but soon would become a Jewish extermination camp, where three million people were murdered or allowed to starve to death.

On October 15, 1940, considering the empire, Hitler decided on the future of the Czechs. Half of them were to be "assimilated" into the German Reich, shipped to

Germany as slave labor. The other half were to be "eliminated."

Meanwhile the Polish and Czech economies would be stripped in the interest of Germany. But the greatest economic prizes were in the highly industrialized countries of Western Europe. The Germans would strip Europe of fifteen trillion (15,000,000,000,000) dollars, of which half would come from France. The Germans would take two-thirds of Belgium's national income, and two-thirds of Holland's. But that was only the official transactions. From the beginning of the occupation, the Germans stripped the other countries of food, clothing, industrial goods, and art. Anything that could be moved usually was.

Hermann Goering was the driving force in the looting of art objects. As soon as Poland was conquered, he moved in to take what he wanted for his private art collection. After the fall of France, he looted the Louvre, first for Hitler's meager needs, then for his own fattening collection, and finally for the German museums. His first loot was loaded into two railroad cars and hooked up to his special train, bound for Berlin.

After France capitulated, her prisoners of war taken by the Germans were not returned home, but thousands of them were carted off to Germany to work as slave laborers in work camps run by the big German industries.

The terror in France did not materialize immediately. In the beginning, the Pétain government had authority over all of France except Alsace and Lorraine, which the Germans annexed, but in fact, the Germans set up an occupation from the Swiss frontier near Geneva to Bourges, to a point east of Tours, and then south to the Spanish frontier at St. Jean Pied-de-Port. That meant Paris and the Channel coast, the Atlantic coast, and the northern industrial areas were all in German hands.

Thus, from the beginning of the Vichy government, there were two Frances—the one centered in the South, where the German pressure was hardly felt, and the France centered on Paris, where the officialdom tended to be more German than the Germans. As journalist-historian Sisley Huddleston put it, "No greater mistake can be made than to confound the two capitals. The Marshal and his government were even more bitterly criticized by the collaborating cliques of Paris, protected by the Germans, and by London or later Algiers."

The ordinary Frenchman was so stunned by the events of the spring of 1940 that he simply turned off and tuned out on the world, occupied himself with making a living and the simple pleasures, and refused to think about past or future.

But the resistance to the Germans, although it had to be quiet and clandestine, began almost from the first. General Weygand went soon to North Africa, to organize an army which in his heart he expected one day to fight the Germans again. Munitions were hidden. The former officers of the army organized themselves into a legion which operated in total secrecy. Youth camps were developed to ally the youth of France with resistance.

Although French resentment against what happened at Mers-el-Kebir was bitter, it soon evaporated when it became apparent that the British were not going to give up, that they would fight the Germans to the bitter end. And that respect brought a kind of sympathy and a belief that the British would in the end win out. As the American sympathy for the British cause became more open and more apparent, French spirits rose again. Hard as life was under the German boot, and it grew increasingly hard, the world had not ended, and Germany had not triumphed.

In the Mediterranean, the first actions in the war after Mussolini joined up on June 10, 1940, hoping to cannibalize France, were air battles between the Italians and the British over Malta. But the war was real if desultory. The British shelled the Italian base at Tobruk on June

12; the Italians retaliated by sinking the British cruiser *Calypso* off Crete with a submarine torpedo. The British bombed Turin and Genoa. With a great flourish, Mussolini began his drive in the Alpine region, and despite a preponderance of six to one against the French there, failed completely. Nevertheless, as noted, Hitler forced the French to sign a separate armistice with the Italians as well, although Italy did not get much out of it. But after that, the war in the Mediterranean became real. In North Africa the Italian military commander was killed by his own antiaircraft guns while flying over Tobruk, and Marshal Rodolfo Graziani became commander of the Italian forces.

In July the Italians advanced from Ethiopia into the Sudan and took Kassala. The British suffered from a shortage of forces; Kassala was defended by only two companies against two Italian brigades. Other Italian forces a few days later moved into Kenya, and the British, outnumbered again, withdrew from the town of Moyale.

In August the Italians invaded British Somaliland with a force of 350,000 troops. The British forces in all of East Africa numbered only 25,000. By midmonth the British were in retreat in Somaliland, and as noted, Churchill blamed General Wavell for the defeat in spite of the great disparity in forces.

On September 6 Grand Admiral Raeder tried to convince Hitler that there was more than one way to defeat Britain. He could see that the Luftwaffe was not able to knock out the British air forces, and he suggested that Hitler think about attacking in the Mediterranean. He tried to expound his strategy, but the army and air force officers made so much fuss that Hitler was distracted.

But three weeks later, when Hitler was beginning to see that Operation Sea Lion had no chance of success, Raeder met with him again, this time privately. The meeting came just after a spectacular British diplomatic and military failure in Africa at Dakar.

In their continued fight against the Germans, Churchill had taken under his wing General Charles de Gaulle, who was regarded in England as the possible rallying symbol of French resistance to the Germans. The British believed that many French officials and soldiers would still fight if given the chance. So in August, as the Battle of Britain was about to begin, Churchill had approved a landing of French and British forces in West Africa, to raise the French flag there and put De Gaulle in power at Dakar. Then De Gaulle would consolidate the French West African colonies, and move up to North Africa, to Morocco, Tunis, and Algeria. The army side of the force would be largely French, but the British navy would transport them.

On the night of August 20, Churchill met with his chiefs of staff and General de Gaulle, and the plan was announced. The British armada would arrive at Dakar in the dawn hours of September 19. Aircraft would drop leaflets over the town, and the British warships would remain on the horizon, while French ships alone would enter the port. A boat carrying a white flag would go into the harbor carrying a letter from De Gaulle. The letter would say that De Gaulle had arrived to save Dakar from imminent German occupation. If the governor agreed to give De Gaulle control, all was well, but if not, the British warships would close in, and if necessary, open fire on the French shore defenses. The plan was designed to produce a De Gaulle coup by nightfall.

Somehow, almost certainly because of treachery within the ranks of the Free French, the plan became known to Vichy, and the French sent three French cruisers and three destroyers to Dakar. British naval intelligence was not functioning very well; the departures were noted by agents, but the messages got lost in the maw of the Admiralty; and so only when the French force was spotted at sea by the British destroyer *Hotspur* on patrol in the Mediterranean was the movement known to London. That was September 11.

The French squadron reached Dakar on September 14. Their arrival reversed the political situation, and Churchill ordered the Dakar plan abandoned. But De Gaulle refused to abandon the plan, and he was backed by the British naval and army commanders involved. So on September 23 the operation began. Two Free French planes landed at Dakar airport, where the pilots were promptly arrested by the Vichy government forces. De Gaulle's emissaries were rebuffed, and later a launch sent into the harbor was fired upon. The British fleet came up to a point three miles off the harbor and began firing. The French replied, and two destroyers were damaged and the cruiser *Cumberland* was badly damaged by a shell that struck in the engine room. The British and French ships then retired.

That afternoon General de Gaulle tried to land his troops, but in fog and confusion, they failed. The commanders asked for advice from London, and Churchill said that having started the affair, they must finish it. "Having begun, we must go on to the end. Stop at nothing."

So that night, De Gaulle sent an ultimatum to the governor of Dakar. The governor replied that he would defend his fortress to the end.

The next morning the British were back, firing, and they engaged the French battleship *Richelieu*. The *Richelieu* was damaged and so was the British battleship *Barham*. The battleship *Resolution* was put out of action for months to come. Nothing was decided. On September 25 the action continued, but since it was obvious that the French would fight to the end, the Churchill cabinet decided to call off the operation.

The meeting between Raeder and Hitler was held in the shadow of this failed action, which proved to Raeder that the British were preparing to move in Africa. Raeder pointed out that the British were now preparing to attack the Italians in the Mediterranean, and quite probably would defeat them without German help. The Italians were loath to let the Germans into their area, but Raeder thought Hitler should insist. It would not be long, said Raeder, before the United States intervened in this war on the side of Britain, and the Germans must secure their southern flank before that time. Raeder gave only until the end of the winter to do this. Gibraltar must be captured, and the Canary Islands secured, as well as the Suez Canal.

Actually this was the same thinking that Churchill was doing about that time. He fully expected a German or Spanish effort against Gibraltar, and was prepared to evacuate the Rock if necessary. But if so, he told the Admiralty, they would have to capture the Canaries, because Britain must have a base from which it could bottle up the Mediterranean.

Hitler promised to think over Admiral Raeder's suggestions. He called in Field Marshal Keitel and told him to go to Italy and offer assistance. Actually Keitel went to Innsbruck and met with Marshal Badoglio, the chief of the Italian General Staff. He offered two German armored divisions for the use of General Graziani, who, in spite of his numerical superiority over the British, was having trouble in Tripolitania. The discussions ranged over the whole gamut of German-Italian war efforts, antiaircraft defenses for Italian war plants, assistance to the Germans in the matter of fuel supplies, and the big problem of Italian armament. The Germans were in the process of assuring fuel supply through Rumania, which had just suffered a revolution, bringing into power the Iron Guard, a fascist and pro-Nazi group. In the end, Badoglio rejected the German offer of troops, claiming that the German panzer divisions would bog down in the African sands. All that could be agreed upon was the dispatch of a team of armored warfare experts under

Colonel Freiherr von Funck to North Africa to study the situation.

As noted, the Italians had offered to put their submarine fleet of more than a hundred, the largest in Europe, at the disposal of the Germans, and Admiral Doenitz had tentatively agreed to a cooperative effort in the Atlantic. Hitler and Mussolini had also agreed to send some German air force units to southern Italy to attack the British convoy traffic and the big base at Malta. This would help protect Italy's communications with the Tripoli expeditionary force, which was suffering from attacks by the British.

Recalling Admiral Raeder's advice, Hitler now began to explore the possibility of staging an attack on Gibraltar. This move would require the acquiescence, if not the help, of Spain.

In September, too, Marshal Pétain was seeking a meeting, hoping to gain German acquiescence to a move of the new French government back to Paris. So in October 1940, Hitler and Field Marshal Keitel boarded the führer's special train and rode to the French-Spanish border town of Hendaye. (Irún is the Spanish town on the other side.)

After the fall of France, Franco, like Mussolini, had wanted to share in the spoils, and he had promised to enter the war on the side of Germany if Hitler would give him the French African empire and would supply Spain with war materials. But this was October 23; all the promises that Britain would be subdued had fallen short, Britain was still very much in the war, the American decisions about massive aid to Britain had been announced, and Generalissimo Franco was having some second thoughts about Hitler's chances of victory.

Hitler did not help anything by prevaricating. He said: "England is already decisively beaten," which Franco could see was not true. When Franco made his request for the French colonies, Hitler said that he would meet the request as far as possible if the French could be given Britain's African colonies in return. This was becoming much too complicated for the Spanish dictator, and he backed off.

Hitler suggested that Spain enter the war in January 1941. Franco said that was too soon.

Hitler asked Franco to attack Gibraltar; the Germans would supply airborne troops, the same troops who had astounded the world by capturing the reportedly impregnable bastion of Fort Eben Emael in Belgium in a few hours. Franco said that if he was going to attack Gibraltar, the task would be undertaken by Spanish troops alone.

They conferred for nine hours, with a break for dinner in Hitler's private railroad car, and nothing was decided. Hitler then left Foreign Minister von Ribbentrop behind to continue the discussions, and he went to Montoire, a railroad station south of Paris, to meet with Marshal Pétain. Ribbentrop continued the arguments for the invasion of Gibraltar, but it was obvious that Franco was determined to stay on the fence. Obviously he did not believe that Hitler would win this war, and so he refused to commit himself to joining the Axis.

At Montoire, Hitler secured Pétain's agreement to join with the Axis in furthering the defeat of England. Collaboration, it was called, thus coining one of the epithets of the occupation of Europe. In return, Hitler promised that France would have a favored place in Germany's "New Europe." He also kept the door open for Franco, noting that France might lose some of her North African colonies (which Franco wanted so much), but that if so, she would be compensated by the gift of British colonies. Hitler wanted more—the active participation of France in the war against Britain—but Pétain sensed the mood of his countrymen and would not go so far. As Sisley Huddleston put it: "A fresh manifestation of admiration for England was indicated everywhere when it became apparent that England would never succumb before the menace of a German invasion. At first, the ordinary man had, for a brief space, deemed it likely that England would fall. Now he saw that she was indomitable. He saw that she would never yield and that whatever happened, she would listen to no overtures of peace, which could only have been at the expense of France. The old conception of England, firm and invincible, in spite of modern weapons, in spite of airplanes, was confirmed.''

The average Frenchman did not know what happened at Montoire, for the agreement between Hitler and Pétain was held in the deepest of secrecy. William L. Shirer called the Montoire meeting "a treacherous act" by Pétain. Huddleston called it a triumph of diplomacy, keeping Hitler at bay with empty promises. In fact, the agreement did not have much substance, and France did not join the Axis in war against England. So Hitler's southern trip was a failure all around, to be followed by another maddening problem engendered by Mussolini.

Hitler and Mussolini had conferred at the Brenner Pass three weeks earlier, but since that time, Mussolini had decided to attack Greece in order to enlarge the Italian Empire. In the aftermath of the French armistice, which had given Italy nothing, and the German political victory in Rumania, which Mussolini also coveted, he was feeling much put upon by his German ally, and so he decided he would not tell Hitler about the Greece venture but present him with a fait accompli.

Hitler came to Florence for this meeting on October 28, and Mussolini greeted him with the glowing report that Italian troops were on the march, crossing the Greek-Albanian border. Hitler grumbled, but there was nothing he could do to stop the foray.

Within a week the Greeks had routed the Italians. Hitler then decided that he had to move in the Mediterranean, as Raeder said. He would send ten divisions into Rumania, and then into Greece through Bulgaria.

On November 4 Hitler met with his top defense officials, and out of the meeting developed a plan for an attack on Gibraltar, the Spanish Canary Islands, and the Portuguese Cape Verde Islands. But Hitler was not really convinced by all Raeder's arguments about the importance of the war in North Africa, and so in the fall of 1940, as Raeder pointed out to Hitler, the opportunity was lost.

CHAPTER 12

The War Shifts South

From Britain's point of view, the fall of France changed the war entirely. Not only were the British standing alone against Hitler, but his new ally Mussolini posed a serious threat to the African empire and the British trade routes to South Africa and Australia and India.

Mussolini was bursting with that ambition for empire that had led him in 1935 to conquer Ethiopia. When he declared war on Britain and France on June 10, he had about 215,000 Italian troops in North Africa, plus the garrisons in the Italian colonies of Ethiopia, Eritrea, and Somaliland. Mussolini's air force also had a vast superiority in numbers of aircraft. The British forces did not amount to much more than 50,000 men, and most of these were concentrated in Egypt, which was the great prize coveted by Il Duce. At the time of the declaration of war, British intelligence knew that Mussolini was gearing up for a major assault on Egypt.

The Italians first moved in three other directions: along the White Nile towards Khartoum; in Kenya, heading toward Nairobi; and in British Somaliland.

But the preparations for the attack on Egypt were much older and much more substantial. Mussolini had built a fine highway, a thousand miles long, which ran along the coast from Tripoli through Tripolitania, Cyrenaica, and Libya to the Egyptian frontier. They had established supply and ammunition dumps at Benghazi, Derna, Tobruk, Bardia, and Sollum, all of these names too soon to become almost household words in Britain.

These bases were jewels; they held the food and the water that would be needed by an army. The road itself traversed desert land, and except for the oases, there was nothing to sustain life along this unfriendly coast. Here by midsummer the Italians had brought perhaps three hundred thousand troops in all, eighty thousand of them very near the Egyptian border. Their goal was the Nile Delta.

The British frontier position against the Italians was the railhead town of Mersa Matrûh, from which an aphalt road ran to Sidi Barrâni. But there was no decent road between Sidi Barrâni and Sollum. It was track and wasteland.

Before the declaration of war, the British war cabinet had warned the chiefs of staff to be ready for immediate action in Egypt, and on the day of the declaration by Italy, the British Seventh Hussars with light tanks and the Eleventh Hussars with armored cars, plus infantry and horse artillery, staged an attack on the Italian frontier posts. Rome had failed to notify Marshal Balbo, the commander of the Italians, that Mussolini was declaring war, and the raid was a complete surprise. So from the beginning, the background of comic opera was apparent in the Italian battle campaign, although it was misleading, for men died and men were wounded and captured by the thousands, because their leaders were inept.

By June 14 the British had captured the frontier posts of Capuzzo and Maddalena, and taken prisoners. On June 16 they intercepted a convoy on the Tobruk-Bardia road, captured a general, and destroyed a dozen tanks. But the Italians reinforced their African forces, and by the middle of July they had recovered their frontier line. The small British force continued to harry the Italians over a sixty-mile front, which was satisfying but could not be decisive. What the action did do was bring attrition to the

Italians: in the first three months, they lost 3,500 men to the British 150.

General Sir Archibald Wavell did not have the forces to launch an assault, so was constrained to wait for the Italians to make a move. The Italian attack was expected to come near Mersa Matrûh.

Prime Minister Churchill took an aggressive stance, although he met opposition all the way. He wanted to arm the Jews of Palestine, and the army fought him. He proposed that most of the twenty-five-thousand-man garrison in Kenya be withdrawn to Egypt. The army balked. He proposed that an amphibious assault be organized to cut the Italian one-thousand-mile road, and the generals grumbled about politicians interfering in their field— which was not quite the case since Churchill was a graduate of the military academy at Sandhurst and had served in several capacities in the army before he became a journalist and politician. He ran into the opposition of Wavell and other generals, who did not want to move troops out of any area that might be threatened. ''Woolly-headedness,'' Churchill called it. His opinion of most of the peacetime generals who were still in command in high places was not very high, and from the outset, then, this opinion applied to General Wavell. The generals balked, but Churchill forged ahead. Singapore was stripped of an Australian division, which was taken to India for hurry-up training and then to head for the Western Desert.

On August 8 Churchill summoned General Wavell to London for conferences. The meetings were not very satisfactory from Churchill's point of view and did not raise his opinion of Wavell. But the commotion in London did have a salutary effect in one way. In spite of the concern for the possibility of a coming German invasion, the War Cabinet agreed to send 150 tanks, antitank guns, antiaircraft guns, and field guns to Egypt to bolster the forces there.

On August 16, 1940, Churchill predicted a major Italian assault on Egypt and warned General Wavell. He called for the deployment of the largest possible army on the Egyptian western frontier. He also set up priorities. The British had been forced to evacuate British Somaliland, which was a painful matter to Churchill, because it raised the world opinion of the Italians and lowered that of Britain, at a time when she needed all the support she could get. Churchill also thought the evacuation was premature and unnecessary.

Originally the British general staff had agreed that in case of war with Italy, British Somaliland would be indefensible, and had planned to evacuate at once. But in December 1939 the chief of staff decided that they would at least hold Berbera. Defenses were ordered for the Tug Argen Gap through the hills. Five battalions of infantry, plus a camel corps and an artillery battery, were gathered in the Berbera region by August 1940. General Wavell indicated that the territory should and would be held. But on August 3 the Italians attacked with three battalions of infantry, fourteen of colonial infantry (black troops, who were regarded as distinctly inferior), pack artillery, tanks, and armored cars. The local British commander, General Godwin Austen, had spoken bravely of defense, but in the event, one key position was captured by the Italians, and four days later General Austen ordered a withdrawal "to save us from disastrous defeat and annihilation." General Wavell authorized the evacuation, and it was carried out under a fighting rear guard action by a battalion of the famous Black Watch Regiment.

Churchill was furious. It was the first (and only) time that the British had been defeated by the Italians. The defeat, coming as it did on the heels of the fall of France and the threat to Egypt, cost the British dearly in prestige throughout the Middle East. Mussolini trumpeted to the skies. Wavell tried to protect General Austen and thus got himself firmly written into Churchill's bad books.

Because of this defeat, Churchill decided the defense of the Sudan would have to come before the defense of Kenya, no matter what the generals said. Kenya could be easily reinforced by sea and rail, whereas the Italians would have to march overland to attack at the Tana River.

Because Britain could expect an air assault on the Red Sea, which was a British lake, the air garrison at Aden would have to be reinforced. The Australians, who had reached Palestine, would be moved to the Nile Delta area. In all, then, the army of Egypt would consist of:

1 British armored force

8 British battalions

3 battalions from the Suez Canal Zone

14 infantry battalions from Palestine

1 New Zealand Brigade

1 Australian Brigade

1 Polish Brigade

½ Union Brigade from East Africa

2 Indian infantry divisions

11,000 replacements to go to Suez

150 field guns

The Egyptian army

All this came to 56,000 men and 212 field guns and the armored forces.

In addition, an armored brigade was to be sent from England through the Mediterranean, although that would be very dangerous, because of the Italian superiority in number of aircraft. In essence, the British would attempt to hold the Mersa Matrûh border position.

Water supplies between Mersa Matrûh and the Alexandria area were to be rendered "depotable"—that is, contaminated to bring confusion to the enemy. The road from Italian Sollum to British Mersa Matrûh was to be wrecked as the troops withdrew along it, by delayed-action mines and chemical destruction of the asphalt surface.

The main line of defense would be along the edge of the cultivated area running from Alexandria. This would be comprised of pillboxes and sandbagged trenches. A strip five miles wide should be flooded from the Nile, controlled at Aswan, said Churchill.

There the Army of the Delta was to await the Italian invasion, which was expected to be powerful, but limited by shortages of water and fuel. An attempt would be made to storm Mersa Matrûh. When the enemy was engaged, Churchill said, the British should then assault his communications by air and from the sea. That was relatively simple, because the communication line was limited to that one lonely narrow strip of asphalt along the coast.

The Churchill plan envisaged a hiatus until October 1, but he admitted they might not have that much time.

This directive was given to General Wavell just before he returned to Cairo in the third week of August.

At sea in the Mediterranean, the Italian fleet was an unknown quantity, although on paper it was very impressive. It included 6 battleships, 19 modern cruisers, 120 destroyers, and more than 100 submarines. The British had a force at each end of the Mediterranean. Force H at Gibraltar included the battle cruiser *Hood*, the battleships *Resolution* and *Valiant*, the aircraft carrier *Ark Royal*, 2 cruisers, and 11 destroyers. At Alexandria lay the Mediterranean Fleet. The British attacked Tobruk from the sea as soon as the war began and sank the Italian cruiser *San Giorgio*. They also destroyed 10 Italian submarines, with a loss of 3 British submarines.

On July 8 Admiral Cunningham was taking a convoy from Malta to Alexandria when he became aware of Italian sea activity. The Italians were trying to lure the

British fleet under the Italian air force and submarines. Cunningham took the initiative and attacked the Italian warships, chasing them and damaging three ships but suffering no damage to British ships. The convoy reached Alexandria safely.

Because the danger of air attack was so great, Churchill insisted on the buildup of the Malta air force. Churchill wanted to send tanks to Egypt, but the Admiralty wanted to send them around the Cape of Good Hope because of the danger of air attack to the convoys. Churchill vetoed this as tying up the tanks for weeks. But ultimately he was forced to accept the longer passage because the Admiralty would not budge from its position. If he had fired Admiral Pound, the chief of the navy, no other admiral would have done the job either. Such were the limitations on even the power of the prime minister.

At the beginning of August 1940 the air defenses of Malta consisted of three ancient Gladiator planes, known locally by the names of Faith, Hope, and Charity. As everyone knew, these tired old aircraft would be but pieces of grist for the Italian air force mill. But that month the resupply of Malta's air power began when the old carrier *Argus* brought twelve Hurricane fighters to a point where they could fly off and reach the island. A second attempt in November was not so successful. Nine of the fourteen planes flown off were lost at sea with their pilots; the distance had been too great and the wind too strong for the four-hundred-mile journey. An overland delivery route was selected, which involved shipping planes in crates to Takoradi in West Africa, and then flying them to Khartoum and Cairo.

The Italian lassitude in Egypt gave the British time, and the British used the time well. They strengthened the Mediterranean Fleet at Alexandria and Force H at Gibraltar. By October 1940 the British had also strengthened the land forces in Egypt, with tanks and infantry. But Churchill was not satisfied with the leadership in the

Middle East, so he sent the Secretary of State for War, Anthony Eden, to make a personal inspection. If Britain was not invaded by the end of October, and Churchill did not now believe she would be, then he wanted to speed the reinforcement of the Middle East.

Eden went south. At Gibraltar he was much impressed by the strength of the defenses and the spirit of the people. On October 15 he reached Cairo and conferred with General Wavell and his staff. He was particularly impressed by General Maitland-Wilson, commander of the Army of the Nile, who vowed to defend the delta successfully. Churchill was pleased when Eden reported that the land had been flooded according to his request and that the defenses were being strengthened all along the delta perimeter.

One thing became apparent in the Eden visit: the role of the tank in desert warfare was much more important than the generals had before believed. General Wavell now asked for more infantry tanks (Matildas).

And not only was the army expanded, but the Mediterranean fleet was strengthened by the addition of the aircraft carrier *Illustrious* and the battleship *Valiant*.

While the British were preparing for war in the desert, they were also looking to the future, when France once more could be considered an ally. In the summer of 1940 Prime Minister Churchill signed a military agreement with General de Gaulle and began working, through the BBC and elsewhere, to increase De Gaulle's prestige in France. In October Churchill addressed the French people in French, promising them to keep fighting, a speech that he delivered in the middle of an air raid. He promised that in 1941 the British would seize command of the air.

He told the French that the Germans would try to obliterate their civilization and called on them to give at least moral support to Britain in her battle.

When Mussolini invaded Greece on October 28, the Greeks called on the British to redeem a promise made by Prime Minister Chamberlain in the spring of 1939. King George of England replied to the king of Greece that Britain would honor her commitment and fight with the Greeks against Italian invasion.

Back in Cairo, Anthony Eden conferred with General Wavell and Admiral Cunningham about the Middle East prospects. Cunningham expected an Italian attack on Crete once Greece was overrun. The men on the scene were reluctant to disperse their forces to help Greece while there was a threat to Egypt. So a squadron of Blenheim bombers was sent to Athens, but nothing more. Then Eden went back to London to deliver to Churchill the very welcome Wavell plan for an offensive to be called Operation Compass.

Marshal Graziani's Italian army of eighty thousand men was spread over a fifty-mile front along the Egyptian border, with no particular order or support system. Between the right flank at Sofafi and the next camp at Nibeiwa was a gap of twenty miles. The British planned to get through this gap and then turn toward the sea, attacking Nibeiwa and other camps from the rear. Meanwhile the Sofafi camps and one at Meiktila would be taken by other British forces. When the British arrived on the sea at BuqBuq, they would cut off three-quarters of Graziani's army from its supply line. Thus would end the Italian assault, with no chance for the Graziani force to retreat to Tripoli.

The British occupied Crete, and Admiral Cunningham hoped to draw out the Italian fleet. He did not succeed, but on November 11, 1940, planes from the aircraft carrier *Illustrious* attacked the Italian fleet at Taranto in the heel of the Italian boot, and disrupted that fleet. This was a historic attack, settling once and for all the question of the effectiveness of aircraft against battleships. Three Italian battleships were put out of commission.

The Allies were winning this round on the land, too. In the Macedonian sector in the third week of November, the Greeks captured Koritza. On the Pindus River, an Italian Alpine division was wiped out. On the coast, the Italians retreated from the Kalamas River, pursued by General Papagos. By the end of the year, the Greeks had pushed the Italians thirty miles beyond the Albanian frontier, along the entire front. Sixteen Greek divisions held down twenty-seven Italian divisions.

In Berlin that fall, it was apparent that something new had to be done to prosecute the war against the British, since Operation Sea Lion had been shelved. The war at sea described in the next chapter was progressing more satisfactorily for the Germans since the fall of France, but the Italian venture into Greece was very unsatisfactory to Hitler, and the Italian campaign in Africa was an unknown quantity, with Marshal Graziani's troops poised but not acting.

On November 4 Hitler held a war council meeting at the chancellery, with General Halder and Field Marshal Brauchitsch from the army, and Field Marshal Keitel and General Jodl from the OKW. It was decided there to wait and see what happened in Egypt before committing troops. All that were committed were some dive-bombers to attack the British fleet at Alexandria and to mine the Suez Canal.

But at this conference the Germans reacted to the British occupation of Crete and Lemnos islands. The Germans agreed that the British now posed a serious threat to the Rumanian oil fields, which were so important, and which could be bombed from the islands. The British alliance with Greece threatened the German opposition in the Balkans.

Hitler was already making his plan for the invasion of Russia, and that presupposed a completely safe Balkan area. So Hitler ordered the army to prepare for invasion of Greece through Bulgaria with at least ten divisions. And the plans for the capture of Gibraltar were laid down.

This move would be called Operation Felix, the capture of "the rock" and the Canary and the Cape Verde islands. Even Portugal might have to be occupied, and if so, the code name would be Operation Isabella. The French fleet would be released, and some French troops, who would be expected to defend the possessions in Northwest Africa. "From this initial task," said Hitler, "France's participation in the war against England can develop fully."

Admiral Raeder was very much concerned about the Italian failures in Greece, and he predicted that the Italians would never carry out the offensive against Egypt. How right he was.

On December 6, 1940, General Wavell uncorked his offensive, having first given an impression of growing weakness because of the dispatch of some troops to Greece. Some twenty-five thousand men moved forward more than forty miles, and on December 7 lay quiet in the desert, unnoticed by the Italian air force. On December 8 they moved up farther, and at dawn on December 9 the battle of Sidi Barrâni began. The first day marked the British attack on Nibeiwa and the Tummar camps. Most of the defenders were captured. The Seventh Armored Division isolated Sidi Barrâni by cutting the coast road. On the morning of the tenth, the Coldstream Guards led an assault against the Italian positions on the Mersa Matrûh front, supported by the guns of the Mediterranean Fleet. They captured prisoners by the thousands, so many that they measured them thus: "There were about five acres of officers and two hundred acres of other ranks."

That afternoon Sidi Barrâni fell. Then the pursuit began. In Berlin, very quietly, Hitler ordered the scrapping of Operation Felix, because the political conditions had changed. The defeat of the Italians in Egypt had made up Franco's mind for him. He would not enter the war on the side of the Germans.

By December 12 most of three Italian divisions had

been killed or captured. General Wavell then prepared to assault the Italians and liberate Ethiopia. By December 15, all enemy forces had been driven out of Egypt, most of five Italian divisions had been destroyed, the Italian forces in Cyrenaica had withdrawn to Bardia, and thirty-eight thousand prisoners had been taken by the British, with casualties of less than five hundred.

The next target of the British was the fortress of Bardia in Libya, with an eighteen-mile belt of modern defenses. An antitank ditch twelve feet wide and four feet deep gave way to a barbed-wire entanglement and concrete bunkers, in two lines, mutually supporting, about eight hundred yards apart. General Bergonzoli, the Italian commander, had forty-five thousand men and four hundred guns. Major General Richard N. O'Connor, the field commander of the British, could mount an assault force about one-third as large in his Thirteenth Corps.

The Sixth Australian Division was chosen to make the assault. The troops had 120 field guns and 23 infantry tanks. The attack began early on the morning of January 3, 1941, when at five-thirty a barrage was laid down and the troops began to move toward Bardia. They blasted their way through the wire and made two lanes for the tanks. Infantry and tanks drove into the town. By half past six, the Italian prisoners were coming in, eight thousand of them by 8:00 A.M. Then the Mediterranean Fleet got into action offshore, and laid down a barrage. RAF planes bombed the Italian airfields nearby. The next day the troops were on the road through Bardia town and the road to Tobruk. The defense was split, and the Australians took the town and the port of Bardia that day. On January 5 the battle was over and General O'Connor was casting his eyes on Tobruk. The Seventh Armored Division was racing toward that fortress city. The prisoners of Bardia were counted up; more than forty thousand men had been killed, wounded, or captured, and the 400 guns, 128 tanks, and 700 trucks had fallen to the British.

So by the end of the first week of January, the British had taken seventy thousand prisoners, and wrecked eight Italian divisions. But in Cyrenaica there remained an Italian army of nearly ninety thousand men and nine hundred guns. In Tripolitania were another ninety thousand men with five hundred guns. General Wavell was aware that his force was desperately thin, and the tanks of the armored units were badly in need of repair. But O'Connor had surrounded Tobruk, and so Wavell reluctantly told him to go ahead and take the place.

But now, the Germans decided they had to take a hand to prevent a debacle. On January 11, a week after the fall of Bardia, Hitler decided to move a panzer division into North Africa to rescue the Italians. The general chosen had begun to make a reputation for himself in the French campaign. His name was Erwin Rommel.

The German buildup in Rumania for the attack on Greece through Bulgaria did not go unnoticed in Athens or in London. Winston Churchill was gearing up to fight in Greece, although General Wavell warned against it. To do so, Wavell said, would imperil the African campaign, which was going so successfully. And if the Germans were intent on sending a major force through Bulgaria to attack Greece, the British did not have the resources in the area to stop them.

Churchill was not listening. He offered troops to the Greeks, but the Greek premier—really dictator—General Metaxas, said that he did not want British troops unless they were willing to go on the offensive, which meant a major effort. Churchill knew that with the British commitments to Africa and home defense, he could not do that, so he withdrew the offer. O'Connor, then, could go ahead with his assault on Tobruk.

Tobruk, which was to become so famous, was not much of a town: a small harbor, a scattering of white buildings with red tile roofs, a few palms in the town square and not another tree in sight, a hotel, a restaurant, and a few shops—that is all there was. The Via Balbia ran through the town, from the east leading to Bardia, to the west leading to Derna.

On January 7 General O'Connor's troops surrounded Tobruk. There, under the Italian command of General Tetassi Manella, was the Twenty-second Italian Corps, thirty-two thousand men with 220 guns and 65 tanks, well supplied and well entrenched.

So he began the siege of Tobruk, which had the usual antitank ditch, barbed wire, and bunkers. O'Connor planned the attack for January 20, 1941, and it was later delayed for twenty-four hours. At 5:40 on the morning of the twenty-first, the assault began with a bombardment and the Australian infantry charged. Some of the Italians were captured before they became aware that an attack was occurring.

At 6:45 the infantry tanks broke through the defenses, and they and the infantry fanned out inside. By nightfall the Italian artillery was quiet and General Manella was a prisoner. By early afternoon of the second day, the Australians were in Tobruk, and the Thirteenth Corps was handling the prisoners and the booty, while the Seventh Armored Division was rushing along the road to the west. There were twenty-five thousand prisoners in the stockade, 208 guns, 23 tanks, and 200 trucks. There was enough food to last that garrison for two months. Also, there was a water distillation plant with the welcome capacity of forty thousand gallons a day.

In Tobruk the British had a new advance base from which to spring their attack to the west. They were on the edge of final victory over the Italians. They would drive on to Benghazi; that was decided by the British chiefs of staff on January 21, the day of the victory at Tobruk.

What lay ahead was the Jebel Achdar, the Green mountain range, a region of fertile land, with broad fields of grain, rocky hills spattered with gray olive trees, the white- and red-roofed houses of the Italian farmers, clustering in handsome villages with green gardens and plenty of water. At the back of the Jebel Achdar stood Benghazi. South of the Jebel Achdar was desert, half a continent of it. The Via Balbia followed the rugged coastline to Syrte, but that was the only road. Shortcuts and isolated villages were reached over tracks so rocky and sandy that the Italians said no modern army could ever move across them.

The Jebel Achdar was better sited for defense than the open desert, for its hills were rugged and broken and offered trouble to tanks and armored cars, and its two gateways funneled travelers and armies alike. On the Italian left lay Derna, which was held by one division, a position of great strength, since it lay in a giant wadi or gulch, that stretched out for twelve miles, with sheer sides up to seven hundred feet in height. On the right was the desert and Mechili, the hub of the track that led south of the Jebel. Here stood General Babini with a powerful force and field guns and seventy tanks.

The Australians moved along the coast road through Gazala, and the Seventh Armored Division went overland to Mechili. On January 24 the Australians reached the outskirts of Derna, and were up against the strong Italian defense there, while the Fourth Armored Brigade neared Mechili and was met by an Italian tank force in a spirited but inconclusive action.

The trouble with fighting in the desert was always the high rate of attrition the desert exacted. Attrition. The Seventh Armored Division's tank force at the moment numbered only seventy; the rest were up for repair. The Italians seemed very formidable here, but General O'Connor noted that the two wings of defense were too far away from each other to make a concerted move. So General O'Connor decided first to attack General Babini at Mechili and then bring the Seventh Armored up against the Italians to sweep south of the Jebel Achdar and outflank the Italians at Derna and Benghazi.

On January 25 he ordered an armored attack that was to be followed by an infantry attack. But the Italians were wise, and on the night of the twenty-sixth, after the British armor had moved into position to launch the attack next morning, General Babini and his force escaped northwest into the Jebel Achdar. The tank men blamed the infantry for not making enough patrols to keep track of General Babini, but the damage was done and could not easily be undone, and it really was not so much damage at that, except for General O'Connor's ego, for the way was now open for the advance on Benghazi. But again the desert had its say. O'Connor's Seventh Armored Division was down to fifty heavy tanks and ninety-five light tanks and did not have enough ammunition or fuel for the long march across the desert. So O'Connor had to wait for supplies and reinforcements. A new regiment arrived from the Second Armored Division, which had just come from England to Egypt, but it had to get up to Mechili, and that would take two weeks.

O'Connor decided to take Derna with the Australian force, and on January 30 he did, and the Australian troops pushed forward toward Giovanni Berta.

O'Connor was still waiting at Mechili for resupply on February 1, when Marshal Graziani, the governor general of Libya and commander in chief of the Italian forces, decided to evacuate Cyrenaica and concentrate on the defense of Tripolitania. The Italians began slipping away; O'Connor knew it from air reconnaissance, but there was nothing he could do about it. Or was there? He did have fifty heavy tanks. The march would be 150 miles over very rough terrain, and it would have to be made at top speed. There would be just enough fuel for the division to start with full tanks and food and ammunition for the march. A convoy of trucks could follow with two days food and water and gasoline, and two refills of ammunition. But that was all. When the British arrived to do battle, they would face a numerically superior Italian force that had not had to march 150 miles across the desert, and a force that theoretically had plenty of ammunition and fuel.

But O'Connor could not bear to see the Italians escaping him, so he sent a battle plan and an emissary to General Wavell, asking permission to move out. The permission was granted. So General Michael Creagh's Seventh Armored Division was ordered to march on February 4 to Solluch on the coast road south of Benghazi. That day at first light the fifty heavy tanks and eighty light tanks started west, through a desert strewn with boulders and interspersed with treacherous soft sand. Tanks began to break down, but after fifty miles the going got easier, but now enormous clouds of dust obscured the view so that parts of the column got lost and joined up late. At 3:00 P.M. the Eleventh Hussars reached Msus, but they were still sixty miles from the good coast road. That day aerial observers reported that the Italian evacuation was moving faster, so that night General Creagh decided to send a second force southwest to the coast to cut them off, and next morning a force headed toward Antelat.

That morning aerial reconnaissance showed that the road south of Benghazi was teeming with Italians driving toward the trap. Creagh's new force entered Antelat, found it deserted, and sent armored cars to Beda Fomm and Sidi Saleh. By noon, artillerymen had come up and they blocked the coast road. At twelve-thirty the first Italian trucks appeared and the trap was closed. The Italians tried to break out, but the British artillery opened fire and a battle of annihilation began.

The Fourth Armored Brigade reached Antelat coming overland; the troops arrived at four-thirty in the afternoon, and they struck the flank of the Italians.

At dawn on February 6 in a torrential rainstorm, the Italians tried to break through the southern British road-block. The Royal Horse Artillery shot them down.

The Italians were caught on a hilly plain between Beda Fomm and the sea, along fourteen miles of road. Low ridges gave cover to the British tanks. All day the Italians tried to blow the British tanks off the road. The British had nineteen heavy tanks and seven light tanks on hand. The Italians had many more, but they were all mixed up with trucks and small vehicles and thousands of infantrymen. By noon, forty Italian tanks had been knocked out of the fighting, but they still had fifty more. The only fifteen British tanks not in action lay at Antelat, paralyzed for want of gasoline.

Thirty Italian tanks that evening broke through the British line and headed toward the armored cars at Antelat. The British stopped all but four of them.

On February 7 the Italians made another desperate attempt to break out; a column of tanks and trucks drove through the British infantry, but the artillery began firing and knocked out all the Italian tanks inside the British camp. That was the end of the Italian Tenth Army. Along fourteen miles of road lay hundreds of Italian tanks and trucks, field guns, and ammunition carriers. The plain was strewn with small arms, and the papers of an army blew around the fields, like small kites caught in the wind. The British had taken twenty thousand prisoners, 112 medium tanks, 216 guns, and 1,500 vehicles. General Tellera was dead, and General Bergonzoli was captured.

So what now? General O'Connor wanted to advance, but when he sent a trusted officer to make the request, and the envoy reached Cairo, he saw in General Wavell's office that the maps of the desert had been replaced by maps of Greece. Churchill had spoken.

The British prime minister was obdurate. The dictator

Metaxas had died on January 29, and his successor had asked the British for help. Churchill was obsessed then as later with the Balkans, and he insisted that the North African battle was over and that the forces be transferred to Greece.

Churchill's military advisers tried to persuade him that at least twenty divisions would be necessary to defend Greece against a major German attack—which was expected—and the British did not have them. Churchill was unmoved, and determined to have a Balkan front. Wavell asked for permission to continue to move in Africa. The British could completely wipe out the Italian presence by taking Tripoli. But Churchill said no. The troops would go to Greece.

And so the victorious British army, which was just short of total victory, was disbanded and turned into a garrison camp. General Erwin Rommel, dispatched with a single German panzer division to shore up the Italians, arrived in Tripoli on February 12. He looked around him at chaos:

"On 8th February," he said, "leading troops of the British army occupied El Agheila. Graziani's army had virtually ceased to exist. All that remained of it were a few lorry columns and hordes of unarmed soldiers in full flight to the west. If Wavell had now continued his advance into Tripolitania, no resistance worthy of the name could be mounted against him."

Thus, with victory within his grasp and full knowing it, General Wavell was forced to abandon the fight and turn toward a Greece that he knew could not be saved from the German threat. The British, forced by Churchill, thus snatched stalemate from the jaws of victory.

For General Rommel had not come down to Africa to supervise the defense of Tripoli, but to win the desert war.

CHAPTER 13

The Battle of the Atlantic Begins

In the first twelve months of the war, the U-boat arm had sunk a British battleship, a carrier, 3 destroyers, 2 submarines, and 5 auxiliary cruisers, plus 353 merchant ships, totalling 1,513,390 tons of shipping. Doenitz had begun the war with 57 U-boats. Twenty-eight U-boats had been lost, but 28 had been commissioned in that year, so the situation was the same.

Actually, for operational purposes, at the beginning of September 1940, Doenitz had fewer boats than a year before, because more boats were undergoing trials and training. Crews had to be trained this autumn for the new boats that would be coming along in the winter under the stepped-up construction program.

Submarines were a dangerous game, and the results so far proved it. Of the boats taking part in operations, 46 percent had been lost. The big change had come in July, when the first U-boats had arrived at Lorient, the new French base. The British were conserving their defenses for the expected invasion of Britain, and the convoys and shipping patrols suffered because of it. Doenitz swiftly recognized a weakening of British defenses, but he could not take full advantage of it, because he did not have the manpower or the boat power at the moment.

Lieutenant Commander Victor Oehrn, the operations

officer of the U-boat arm, had almost single-handedly restored the morale of the U-boat force that spring, as the German army rolled through France and created a whole new war for the U-boats, by taking control of the French ports.

Oehrn had gone out in May, when the U-boat operations had come to a virtual standstill because of the problems with the torpedoes. His *U-37* had arrived on station off Cape Finisterre on May 18. The next day Oehrn fired five magnetic torpedoes, four of which failed. This was what Doenitz wanted to know. The fifth torpedo sank the Swedish motorship *Erik Frisell*. So this was the problem in a nutshell, 20 percent effectiveness. No wonder the U-boat captains were discouraged by their lack of results and irritated by the Doenitz staff, which had been inclined to blame the torpedo failures on human error.

After the first day, Oehrn deactivated his magnetic torpedoes and used them as contact exploders. The results were spectacular:

May 22 damaged 9,400-ton British motorship *Dunster Grange*

May 24 sank 4,000-ton Greek steamer *Kyma*

May 27 sank 5,000-ton British steamer *Sheaf Mead*

May 27 sank 3,400-ton Argentine freighter *Uruguay*

May 28 sank 10,000-ton French motorship *Brazza*

May 28 sank 500-ton French trawler *Julien*

May 29 sank 2,500-ton French steamer *Marie Jose*

On May 29, Oehrn ran out of torpedoes. But he still had time left on his cruise, and he decided to stay out and use his deck gun. In the next few days he gunned down the 7,400-ton British tanker *Telena*, the 950-ton Greek steamer *Ioanna*, and the 2,300-ton Finnish steamer

Snabb. Then he sailed back to Wilhelmshaven, having sunk eleven ships with a tonnage of 44,000.

All the old enthusiasm of the U-boat skippers was restored. Now, when they went out, however, it would be a different story.

In the summer of 1940 as the British gathered their naval forces together around the British Isles, prepared to repel the German invasion they expected, the pickings for the submarines got better. More ships were sailing without escort, outside convoys, and individual ships were easy targets. A skipper on the Atlantic run down to Gibraltar had an easy time of it, potshotting at individual ships as they came by.

But Doenitz was preparing for something new that fall, the perfection of the wolf pack technique. The capture of France and French naval ports had brought some welcome intelligence to the Germans. As noted earlier, Churchill had made it certain the French navy was instructed in the use of the asdic underwater sound ranging system, as an antidote for U-boats. With the fall of France, the Germans had thrust into their hands complete information on the asdic systems, making it much easier for them to find antidotes. The wolf pack system was going to lend itself to obviating the asdic system, too, because with a whole flotilla of U-boats on the attack, the escorts would be hard put to make sense of their echo ranging.

In that summer of 1940, Doenitz transferred most of his U-boat command functions from Wilhelmshaven to France, and prepared to put the wolf pack system to the test.

One of Doenitz's prime weapons was an excellent system of communications and a grid map of the world's waters, so that he could locate and direct his U-boats easily. From his communications center, be it at Wilhelmshaven or Lorient, south of Brest, he ran his

U-boats as a conductor runs an orchestra, with tight control.

July 1940, Doenitz observed, marked the beginning of the first phase of the Battle of the Atlantic. In June 1940 the western end of the English Channel was still the focal point of British sea traffic, until the fall of France put the French ports into German hands, and then the British switched their convoy routes to south of Ireland up to the north and into the North Channel.

But there simply were not enough escorts to go around, and so from May until October 1940, outward-bound convoys were escorted only as far as twelve degrees west longitude. At these points the homeward-bound convoys were picked up by the escorts and taken into port.

Convoys from Canada and the United States were escorted by Canadian destroyers for four-hundred miles eastward into the Atlantic, but then the escort had to turn back, and the convoy would then be protected either by a single escort or, as likely, an auxiliary cruiser or armed merchant vessel.

There was really not much to be done in the face of the German invasion threat that summer, but a new base could be established, and was, in the British occupation of Iceland, the Danish colony. Actually, Hitler had planned to occupy Iceland himself, but the British beat him to it.

These changes did not help the British too much. Doenitz's men quickly discovered the new convoy routes. What Doenitz wanted was to make concentrated assaults on the convoys with a number of boats.

In that summer of 1940, German surface raiders captured several British merchant ships and in their papers found copies of the merchant ship signal codes and instructions to merchant ships. The Germans had broken the code that the British were using to route their convoys, and so Doenitz tried to make contact with convoys through deciphered messages. But the British foxed him by changing the rendezvous points for several convoys, and so the U-boats went empty-handed in their attempts between June and September.

The failure to find the convoys, however, did not mean the Germans were not sinking ships.

"If even two days passed without my receiving reports of ships having been sighted by U-boats, I at once ordered a redistribution of my forces," Doenitz wrote. "As it became more and more evident that we stood an excellent chance of achieving really great successes, I was most anxious that not one single day should pass without the sinking somewhere or other of a ship by one of the boats at sea."

Only on four days of the month of June did Doenitz's captains disappoint him. The total sinkings for the month was sixty-four ships, totalling 260,478 tons. It was the most successful month for the U-boats since the opening of the war.

So numerous did the U-boat successes become that a whole corps of "star" captains emerged, to be lionized by Dr. Goebbels's propaganda machine. Lieutenant Engelbert Endrass in *U-46* sank six merchant ships on one patrol. Lieutenant Hans Jenisch in *U-32* sank five ships. But the greatest ace was still Guenther Prien. On June 10 he sailed on patrol and sank ten ships.

After Lorient became operational for the U-boats, in July 1940, the sinkings increased. Although in August the tonnage was down from 267,000 to 214,000 tons, Admiral Forbes, the director of antisubmarine warfare for the Royal Navy, protested that the fleet had taken too many of his antisubmarine vessels and was making protection of convoys more difficult all the time.

To add to the British troubles was the specter of the Italian submarine fleet, over one hundred strong, which was offered to the Germans. The first Italian submarines to go out from German bases were the *Malaspina* and the *Dandolo*, and they added to the total sinkings. The

Dandolo sank two ships on her first cruise from a French port.

In September 1940 Doenitz got his first big break. He had a four-day warning about the coming of a fifty-one-ship convoy from Canada. The convoy had been escorted out into mid-Atlantic by Canadian destroyers and would be picked up near the British coast by British destroyers. But there was this wide stretch of the Atlantic to be navigated with minimal escort. The British planned to pick up the convoy at twelve degrees west longitude, so Doenitz planned to pick them up first at nineteen degrees west longitude. Lieutenant Commander Prien's *U–47* would lead the pack.

Prien was out looking already. On September 2 he sank the six-thousand-ton Belgian steamer *Ville de Mons*, which was traveling unescorted from New York to Belfast. On September 4 he sank the nine-thousand-ton British steamer *Titan* from Convoy OA207, outbound from Britain.

Then Admiral Doenitz instructed Prien to pick up Convoy SC2—nine columns of ships traveling to England. The convoy had picked up its escorts. Prien picked up the convoy about a hundred miles east of the British shore. The weather was overcast, and the swell was heavy, all very well for a submarine and all very difficult for the defenders. Also that night there was no moon.

Prien tracked the convoy for several hours, and at eleven-thirty that night, he attacked. The first the British knew of it was when the destroyer *Lowestoff* sighted a light on the starboard side of the convoy. The captain ordered the destroyer *Scarborough* to take over the convoy and went to investigate, swept completely around the convoy, but made no contact with any submarine.

The *Scarborough* remained out in front of the convoy—the preferred position when there was a single escort, because at least she could keep the U-boats from shooting "down the throat" of the convoy. Just after midnight the *Scarborough* made contact with a submarine, moved until she was four-hundred yards away, when suddenly a gray shape slid into the sea and disappeared. Prien had escaped the destroyer. The *Scarborough* attacked with one depth charge. But the problem of the British then was that setting off a depth charge knocked out their asdic receivers, usually for fifteen or twenty minutes. By the time the asdic was working again, there was no contact.

So Lieutenant Commander Prien was out there somewhere near the convoy, and the two destroyers could not do much about it. It had taken the *Lowestoff* two hours to make the circuit of the convoy, and then to get back into position. A force of two destroyers obviously was not adequate protection for a convoy, but it was all the British could spare these days of peril at home.

At 3:45 the captain of the *Lowestoff* heard another explosion, this time on the port side of the convoy. The destroyer swept along the side, but made no contact. Not until morning did anyone know what had happened. Then a ship count revealed two ships missing. Actually, three ships were missing; the error was that of the convoy commander. The *Neptunian*, *Jose de Larinaga*, and *Gro*, each about five thousand tons, had been lost. They had been sunk by Prien, and the next day he also sank the *Passidon*, and the *U–28* sank the *Mardinian*.

So two submarines in a twenty-four-hour period had sunk five ships from one convoy. That performance pleased Admiral Doenitz, and indicated a fine future for the wolf packs.

When the convoy arrived in Britain, it became obvious that the convoy system had not kept up with modern developments. None of the ships of the convoy had made a signal of any sort. That dark night when the first three ships were sunk, no one had seen anything. But the next day, when the other two ships were lost, men aboard the ship *Sherbrooke* had seen the *Passidon* hit and had not reported it, because they had been told not to. Two other ships had seen the incident of the *Mardinian*, but they had not reported either. Actually, thirty-one survivors in a boat were picked up by the ship *Apollo*, but again she had observed radio silence as demanded, and so no one knew anything about the losses until the convoy arrived in port.

The convoy commander had ordered two emergency turns, and these had been made, but no information about the enemy had reached the escorts. Nor had any of the ships near the stricken vessels made any communication. Something had to be done to improve communications if the U-boat menace was to be countered. The demand for radio silence had been so strongly enforced that it now threatened the whole system. So the British began to change. If a ship was attacked, then the convoy escort commander and the convoy leader should be informed, either by Aldis lamp signal, by flags, or if necessary, by radio. The danger, of course, was that a radio transmission might attract more U-boats like honey attracts flies, but unless the escorts knew what was happening in the convoy, they could not do much to stop it.

After the attack on Convoy SC2, Lieutenant Commander Prien was down to one torpedo. He wanted to go back to Lorient and reload. But Admiral Doenitz needed a weather ship, because a new wrinkle had been added. The Luftwaffe squadron of scout bombers had finally gotten into action, and would cooperate with the U-boats in attacks on convoys. Doenitz had to give them weather reports and convoy information, and he also needed an experienced skipper to scout for the wolf pack he was organizing. So Prien was told to stay out and directed by Doenitz where to go, based on the German intercepts of British messages.

The U-boats began taking ships out of every convoy that came along. On September 15 they attacked Convoy SC3 and sank four ships. Two days later they took two ships from eastbound convoy HX71, and on September 20 they sank four ships from Gibraltar-bound convoy OB216. Then came Convoy HX72.

HX72 was a slow convoy, her speed set at eight knots to accommodate the slowest vessel. The convoy was bound from Halifax, Nova Scotia, to England. On the evening of September 21, the convoy reached the Western Approaches to Britain and was picked up by the team led by the *Lowestoff*, three destroyers and three armed trawlers. Commander A. M. Knapp of the *Lowestoff* was in charge of the convoy protection. Because of his experience with Convoy SC2, he had made some rules. Any escort that witnessed an attack on a ship was to act immediately, fire a gun and send up a rocket to alert the convoy and the other escorts, and then carry out a sweep search for the submarines, firing star shells away from the convoy to confuse the U-boat commander and perhaps to illuminate the U-boat.

In Doenitz, Commander Knapp had a formidable opponent, for that is who was masterminding the convoy attack from his headquarters at Lorient. Here is a report from Doenitz's war diary:

In attacking Convoy SC on September 10, *U–47* had expended all torpedoes but one. His boat was therefore detailed to meteorological duties, sending in reports twice every 24 hours from west of 23 degrees west, which were urgently needed for German air raids on Britain. Although the British Direction Finding Service could presumably plot the position of the U-boat twice daily, Convoy HX72 did not avoid Prien . . .

Route instructions for a British convoy—picked up at this time by the German Intercept Service—seemed to tally with this convoy, for the course was the same as reported by Prien. On this assumption, five boats (*U–99, U–65, U–48, U–46, U–43*) were directed to take up certain positions, through which the convoy would pass at daybreak on the following day. The order was soon canceled when, during the night, the convoy altered course to the southeast, presumably because the radio traffic of the shadower had been intercepted. Operating directly on the shadower's reports, *U–48* came up and fired all her torpedoes while Prien, having no torpedoes, continued to shadow for the oncoming boats . . .

Here is the course of events, according to Commander Knapp's reports.

The weather was terrible from the convoy commander's point of view; the moon shone down brightly on the ships until finally some relief came in the way of rain squalls. At about ten-thirty that evening, a star shell was fired over the starboard side of the convoy. It was a German star shell. A few seconds later, Commander Knapp saw a red light go up on the starboard side of the convoy, which meant one ship had been torpedoed. Commander Knapp was on the port side of the convoy, and he swung out and around and finally saw the torpedoed ship near the center of the convoy.

In rapid succession two more ships were torpedoed, one near the front and another near the rear of the convoy—which meant several U-boats. Several captains recognized this and panicked and the convoy split in two. Ships began scattering, and thus Commander Knapp's shepherding job became impossible.

At midnight he saw a ship go up in flames. He rushed to the area and fired star shells but saw nothing. Then he lost control of the convoy and could not find what was left of it.

Someone reported a submarine on the surface four miles to the northwest. Commander Knapp went to the area, but saw nothing. He had to try to pull the convoy together, but there was no way to do it. Having scattered, they could not be brought together again, for there was no coordination of movement. They were like sheep flying off in all directions when beset by wolves. Knapp did come upon the *Collegian*, which was just then being shelled by the *U–32*, but when he got there, the ship was gone (sunk), and the submarine was gone, too. Two other destroyers came up, and they made a submarine contact. They all began to drop depth charges, which knocked out their asdic echo rangers. They were then "blind" for nearly half an hour, and when they had asdic again, there was no contact.

Thus were the British made alive to the new technique of the wolf pack. They had never heard of the term, and in London there was no recognition of the concept, but Commander Knapp knew. He also knew of another new German technique: operation of U-boats on the surface, around and even inside the convoy.

Of the thirty-seven ships of Convoy HX72, Doenitz's U-boats sank fourteen in two nights. Prien sank one with his one torpedo. Lieutenant Commander Otto Kretschmer sank three ships. *U–48* sank two ships, bringing its total for this single patrol to nine merchant ships and a patrol boat. The *U–100* sank most of all in this convoy, eight ships. *U–32* sank the one, the *Collegian*.

The U-boat war had entered a new and most dangerous phase. By the end of the month, Doenitz reported that his captains had sunk fifty-nine ships, for a total of 295,000 tons.

The increase in production of U-boats and the cutback in travel time to the war zone achieved by the use of the French bases made it possible for Doenitz to keep more submarines at sea for longer periods of time. He now had about thirty operational boats at any given moment, with half of them at sea.

So that summer and fall were to be dark days for Britain in many a way. As far as U-boats were concerned, the Royal Air Force was just beginning to learn. The Admiralty had been after them for months to learn how to use depth charges and depth bombs against submarines, but the RAF had blithely ignored the question. Now Prime Minister Churchill took a hand, and made it crystal-clear to the RAF that they were going to have to comply with Admiralty directives in the interest of the common defense.

What was needed, and no one knew it more clearly than Prime Minister Churchill, were more escorts. The building program was moving apace, as was the Canadian program of building small, lightweight corvettes, and the Americans were beginning to produce some warships for Britain. The fifty overage American destroyers were being converted for Atlantic sea duty, but they were not yet available. And meanwhile Doenitz's wolf pack program was getting into gear.

September was a dreadful month for ship sinkings, but October opened with equally savage and successful attacks. On October 9 Convoy SC6 from America was attacked by two U-boats, and three ships were lost. In the next week, three more convoys were attacked, and lost ten more ships. Then came the story of SC7, bound east for England and loaded with military supplies for the British war effort.

The British still had not caught on to the breach of their convoy decodes by the Germans, so Admiral Doenitz had advance warning once more of the coming of the convoy. On this occasion he was able to assemble a seven-boat wolf pack. Even so, it was not quite as simple as it sounded, because a British convoy commander had the right to alter course, speed, and direction if he thought his charges were in danger, and so some U-boats had to find the convoy even after Doenitz had most of the information about where it should be at any given time.

Lieutenant Heinrich Bleichrodt in *U–48* was selected this time to find the convoy for the wolf pack. Once he radioed back the information, Doenitz could triangulate the source of his broadcast with another U-boat in a different location and a shore station. Then he would put all the information down on his grid board, and move his U-boats around to attack.

Bleichrodt was out searching on the morning of October 15, but had not made contact. The *U–124* found a straggler from this convoy and sank her. She was the Canadian steamer *Trevisa*. Doenitz now at least had a clue as to the general area in which he would find the convoy.

On October 16 Bleichrodt was moving in his general patrol area south of Iceland.

Here is Admiral Doenitz's report from the war diary:

On the night of 16 October, *U–48* in her attack area northwest of Rockall Bank made contact with a homeward-bound convoy. Five more boats lying east and north of Rockall were sent to operate against it. *U–48* attacked on the same night but lost contact after being pursued with depth charges. The other boats were ordered to search along the general line of advance of the convoy toward the North Channel.

On the evening of October 17 another boat (*U–38*) reported having sighted the convoy on the previous night, but to the north of the assumed line of advance. The boats were now uncertain as to the situation and they were ordered to form a patrol line just east of Rockall Bank by the morning of October 18. The convoy would have to pass this way during the hours of daylight. No contact was made by noon . . . The U-boat command immediately sent an amended disposition:

"Proceed to the north to operate against the last position reported."

However, the boats did not need to execute this order as the convoy now ran into the patrol line. The ensuing night brought the enemy his worst losses of the whole campaign, for according to British Admi-

ralty figures, no less than 20 ships fell victim to the
U-boat torpedoes . . .

From the eighteenth the battle continued, with Doenitz
directing it all the way.

Lieutenant Kretschmer's *U-99* was involved in the
conflict. Here is the extract from her war diary to describe
the battle:

October 18.

2 A.M. On receipt of the urgent message To:
U-100, *U-28*, *U-123*, *U-101*, *U-99*, and *U-46*: Be
in position in patrol line from naval grid square 2745
to naval grid square 0125 AM by 8 A.M. I proceed to
my position at maximum speed, although I cannot
arrive until 11 A.M. I therefore report by short signal
to flag officer U-boats, owing to position, cannot comply with dispositional order. My position is naval grid
square 41 AM (a hundred miles southwest of the new
position).

9:03. Sight a U-boat conning tower, bearing 60 degrees. Shortly afterwards a medium boat appears on
the horizon proceeding in a northwesterly direction. It
must be *U-46*, the boat on the left flank of the patrol
line.

11:28 A.M. In position. Proceed up and down across
the patrol line. Medium U-boat in sight. It must be
U-101, which is proceeding up and down along the
patrol line.

12:08. Radio message. To flag officer U-boats from
U-38. Convoy in 1539 AM at 2 A.M. (This is one
hundred miles northwest of the patrol line.) That
means that the convoy will pass the patrol line to the
north. At 3:30 P.M. the patrol line is canceled by radio
from the flag officer U-boats. *U-100*, *U-123*, *U-101*,
U-46 are told to operate on *U-38*'s report. (This is
thirty miles north of the patrol line.)

Flag officer U-boats cannot suppose that *U–99* is on the patrol line. I proceed in an east-northeasterly direction.

5:45 P.M. Wind southeast Force 3, sea 3, moderate cloud. *U–101*, which is two or three miles north, signals by searchlight, enemy sighted to port.

5:49 P.M. A warship is sighted bearing 030 degrees, steering east. Soon afterwards smoke to left of her. Finally the convoy. While ahead to attack, we sight a steamship in the southeast, apparently on a westerly course.

7:28 P.M. Submerge to attack.

7:50 P.M. Surface, as the ship is making off slowly to the east. Haul farther ahead. At 8 P.M. pass within a few hundred meters of a U-boat on the surface, apparently *U–100* again.

8:24 P.M. Another U-boat has torpedoed the ship. Shortly afterwards exchange recognition signals with *U–123*. Convoy again in sight. I am ahead of it so allow my boat to drop back, avoiding the leading destroyer. The destroyers are constantly firing star shells. From outside I attack the right flank of the first formation.

10:02 P.M. Weather. Visibility moderate, bright moonlight. Fire bow torpedo by director. Miss.

10:06. Fire stern torpedo by director. At 700 meters, hit forward of amidships. Vessel of some 6,500 tons sinks within 20 seconds. I proceed head-on into the convoy. All ships are zigzagging independently.

10:30 P.M. Fire bow torpedo by director. Miss because of error in calculation of gyro angle. Therefore decide to fire the rest of the torpedoes without the director, especially as the installation has still not been accepted and adjusted by the Torpedo Testing Department. Boat is soon sighted by a ship which fires a white star and turns toward us at full speed, continuing even after we alter course. I have to make off with engines all out. Eventually this ship turns off, fires one of her guns, and again takes her place in the convoy. I now attack the right flank of the last formation but one.

11:30 P.M. Fire bow torpedo at a large freighter. As the ship turns toward us, the torpedo passes ahead of her and hits an even larger ship after a run of 1,740 meters. This ship of some 7,000 tons is hit abreast the foremast, and the bow quickly sinks below the surface, as two holds are apparently flooded.

11:55. Fire a bow torpedo at a large freighter of some 6,000 tons at a range of 750 meters. Hit abreast foremast. Immediately after the torpedo explosion there is another explosion with a high column of flame from the bow to the bridge. The smoke rises some 200 meters. Bow apparently shattered. Ship continues to burn with a green flame. [ammunition ship].

Skipper Kretschmer then kept after the convoy.

12:15 A.M. Three destroyers approach the ship and search the area in a line abreast. I make off at full speed to the southwest and again make contact with the convoy. Torpedoes from the other boats are constantly heard exploding. The destroyers do not know how to help and occupy themselves by constantly firing star shells, which are of little effect in the bright moonlight. I now start to attack the enemy from astern.

1:38 A.M. Fire bow torpedoes at large, heavily laden freighter of about 6,000 tons, range 945 meters. Hit abreast foremast. The explosion sinks the ship.

1:55 A.M. Fire bow torpedo at the next large vessel of some 7,000 tons. Range 975 meters. Hit abreast foremast. Ship sinks within forty seconds.

2:40 A.M. Miss through aiming error with torpedo fired at one of the largest vessels in the convoy, a ship of the *Glenapp* class of 9,500 tons.

2:55. Again miss the same target from a range of about 800 meters. No explanation as the fire control data were absolutely correct. Presume it to be a gyro failure as we hear an explosion on the other side of the convoy some seven minutes later.

0312. Third attempt at the same target from a range of 7,720 meters. Hit forward of the bridge. Bow sinks rapidly level with the water.

3:56 A.M. Fire at and miss a rather small, unladen ship which had lost contact with the convoy. We had fired just as the steamer turned toward us.

3:58 A.M. Turn off and fire a stern torpedo from a range of 690 meters. Hit aft of amidships. Ship drops astern, somewhat lower in the water. As torpedoes have been expended, I wait to see if she will sink further before I settle her with gunfire.

5:04. Ship is sunk by another vessel by gunfire. I suppose it is a British destroyer, but it later transpires that it was *U–123*. Some of the shells land very close so that I have to leave the area quickly. The ship was the *Clintonia*, 3,106 tons.

5:30. I commence return passage to Lorient.

In two days, six U-boats had sunk twenty-three ships, and this convoy lost twenty-seven ships in all, for a total 105,000 tons. That sort of loss was crippling to the British war effort, obviously, and could not be permitted to go unchallenged.

But with the new bases, and the pressures, it was hard to stop the U-boats. On October 19 Lieutenant Commander Prien's *U–47* encountered Convoy HX79 farther to the west. It also was bound from Halifax to England. With four other U-boats, Prien attacked that night. The attacks went on for three days, and in the end the wolf pack sank fourteen ships from this convoy.

So two major wolf pack attacks had been carried out, and they had given the U-boats a total of sixty ships for the month. Altogether, counting individual sailings and three ships sunk by the Italians, who were just getting into the submarine war, the U-boats sank seventy-eight ships in October.

That news shook the British to the degree that all sorts of new approaches were suggested to fight the U-boat menace. For the first time the submarines were attacking convoys on the surface, where they were much more maneuverable. If the British had adequate air cover, the submarines would also be much more vulnerable, but at this stage, the dice were loaded for the U-boats, not the defenders.

By the end of 1940, Prime Minister Churchill was really worried about the U-boat menace, and in a letter to President Roosevelt, Churchill predicted that 1941 would be a crucial year in the war against Germany. He was no longer worried about invasion, but about the ability of Britain to keep the island supplied from the sea. In the five weeks that ended November 3, he said, Britain's losses at sea, at 420,000 tons of shipping, were comparable to the worst full year of the 1914–1918 war.

The letter was a cry for help.

CHAPTER 14

Struggle at Sea

The help Prime Minister Churchill called on America for at the end of 1940 was already on the way. Fortified by a victory in the presidential election and secure in office for four more years, President Roosevelt went on vacation at sea aboard the USS *Tuscaloosa*, and there with adviser Harry Hopkins, worked out a program of Lend-Lease, which would enable the United States government legally to assist Britain in a new way.

Under the neutrality legislation in force in 1940, the American government was supposed to take a hands-off attitude toward the war in Europe. Private business could supply goods to a belligerent, but only for cash, and only if the goods were shipped in other than American vessels. Both conditions were growing harder for Britain to meet; she was losing shipping rapidly to the U-boats, and the British cash and credits in the United States were vanishing rapidly. Engaged in a total war, the British government and people required the total manufacturing capacity of British industry and more, so the British economy was a deficit economy.

What Britain needed was supply and credit, and Roosevelt proposed to provide both. Under his plan, the American economy was about to embark on a revolutionary military defense program, but would allow Britain as much of American production as could be spared on a loan basis. The provision for repayment of the loans was to be left vague and settled in the future.

This arrangement seemed eminently fair to the British, who held that if the Americans, with their enormous productive capacity, would give them what Churchill called "the sinews of war," they would fight the battle.

There was lively opposition in America to the Lend-Lease program and the new defense effort, but Roosevelt had been elected by a comfortable majority—449 electoral votes to 82—and the Democratic party controlled substantial majorities in both houses of Congress—66 to 30 in the Senate, and 268 to 167 in the House of Representatives. So after the extensive debate, in March 1941 the Lend-Lease Act became law. It was not any too soon, because the German effort in the Battle of the Atlantic had become alarmingly successful.

Meanwhile Roosevelt had set the stage for American military cooperation with Britain. In July 1940 he had issued instructions that resulted in the navy, the army, and the army air corps sending observers to London to work out methods of helping the British. By December the American navy was planning to become involved in escort of convoys, and on January 17 the navy announced that it would be ready to participate in escort as of April. A few weeks later, the American Atlantic Fleet was created, with Admiral Ernest J. King as commander.

As the year 1940 drew to a close, the shipping situation of the British became very grim. And it was not just the U-boats that were taking their toll. During the summer of 1940, Admiral Raeder had fitted out a number of raiders that had their own reconnaissance aircraft. Five of these ships got through the British blockade into the Atlantic, while a sixth negotiated the Northeast Passage behind a Russian icebreaker and went through the Bering Sea into the Pacific. By the first week of September, these ships were raiding British commerce. Two of them were working the Atlantic, two the Indian Ocean, and two the Pacific. They were virtually unseen, and until the end of September, they took thirty-six ships, for a total of 235,000 tons of shipping.

Also by the end of October 1940, the pocket battleship *Scheer* was ready for service, and she left Germany on October 27 and broke out into the Atlantic through the Denmark Strait. A month later the eight-inch gun cruiser *Hipper* also was out. On the afternoon of November 5, the *Scheer* encountered the convoy HX84, which consisted of thirty-seven ships. They were escorted by the single armed merchant cruiser *Jervis Bay*, which was traveling in the middle of the convoy. The captain of the *Jervis Bay* reported the presence of the pocket battleship by radio and then moved into action at full speed while the convoy scattered. The *Scheer* opened fire at eleven miles. The *Jervis Bay*'s 1918 vintage guns would not reach so far, and the one-sided battle began. It lasted for an hour until the *Jervis Bay* was a flaming hulk, abandoned by her crew. Then the *Jervis Bay* sank, carrying down her captain and two hundred men.

The *Scheer* set out after the convoy, but it had scattered and the warship found only a few vessels to attack. Those vessels, however, added up to enough to give her credit for forty-seven thousand tons of ships. Then the *Scheer* hurried south to escape the great sea hunt that was launched for her after the *Jervis Bay*'s report. On November 24 the *Scheer* appeared in the West Indies, where she sank a ship; she remained out, fueled by ships sent from Germany, until April 1941, and accounted for sixteen ships—ninety-nine thousand tons of shipping.

But, troublesome as the raiders were, because they required a heavily disproportionate search force, the big problem for Britain was still the U-boat. Said Churchill:

"A far greater danger was added to these problems. The only thing that really frightened me during the war was the U-boat peril. Invasion, I thought, even before the air battle, would fail. After the air victory it was a good battle for us. We could drown and kill this horrible foe in circumstances favorable to us, and, as he evidently realized, bad for him. It was the kind of battle which in the cruel conditions of war, one ought to be content to fight. But now our lifeline, even across the broad oceans and especially in the entrances to the island, was endangered. I was even more anxious about this battle than I had been about the glorious air fight called the Battle of Britain.''

After the fall of France, and the investment by the Germans of the French seaboard from Dunkirk to Bordeaux, all the supplies coming into Britain had to come around Northern Ireland, in the Mersey and the Clyde rivers. These Churchill called ''the lungs through which we breathed.'' On the east coast and in the English Channel, small vessels moved, under increasing attack from the air and from German E-boats and mines. In the fall of 1940 the situation became grim indeed.

Churchill estimated that in 1941 Britain would need forty-three million tons of imports, and the Doenitz efforts had cut the incoming tonnage to a rate of thirty-seven million. If this was not changed, it would mean real deprivation for the people of England. From the U-boat skipper's point of view, the period July to October 1940 was called ''the happy time''; although Doenitz was puzzled by the ineffectiveness of the British anti-submarine defenses, he was grateful. The only U-boat losses in the month of August came from British mine-laying and British submarines. Doenitz's perception of the escorts was that they were very few, and that was a correct assumption. The Germans did not realize how many British destroyers had been sunk and damaged in Norway and during the days of Dunkirk. The Admiralty was conserving all it could for the possible invasion of Britain, so much of the escort duty was taken over by aircraft, short-range patrol planes, and Sunderland flying boats for longer range. Neither was very effective at this stage, although the Sunderlands, with their bigger bomb capacity, did keep the U-boats pinned down in the North Channel, the principal entry to the British Isles during most daylight hours.

The most dangerous region for the U-boats was that part of the British blockade in the North Sea from Helgoland up the Scandinavian coast, where the British had laid mines and where a number of British submarines operated. Several U-boats were lost here, although the U-boat command kept changing the routes into the North Sea.

The British were immediately aware of the great advantage offered the U-boat force by the possession of the French ports, and they undertook to bomb the submarine pens. The big error of the RAF in this regard was delay. Aerial observation showed that construction of facilities had begun in Norway and in France immediately after the areas were occupied, but the RAF waited to do its bombing on the theory that it was better to destroy an early completed installation than to impede progress. This error made it possible for the Todt organization to build superbly protected pens, which could and did withstand the force of two-thousand-pound bombs time and again. Although the bombing began in a few months, it was totally unsuccessful, and the Germans enjoyed safety in their submarine pens until deprived of them by the Allied successes in France in 1944.

The British tried also to close the French ports by submarine, and in September 20, on leaving Lorient, *U–58* was attacked by a submarine. The same day the catapult ship *Ostmark* was torpedoed. Next day *U–138* was attacked by four torpedoes, and on October 15, *U–645* was attacked just outside Lorient.

The Germans then began to escort all their submarines to deep water.

Doenitz was frustrated that summer, because he knew as well as Churchill that here was the golden opportunity for the U-boats to knock Britain out of the war. The

American aid program had not yet become effective, and the British shortage of escorts and aircraft was serious. But the fact was that in the fall of 1940, Doenitz had fewer U-boats available to him than he had the year before, because the U-boat building program had not yet responded sufficiently, and losses were occurring.

The admiral's problems were increased by Goering's attitude. He was so preoccupied with the Battle of Britain and the Blitz that he gave only lip service to the promise to take care of the U-boat arm's needs for reconnaissance. Therefore, by the end of 1940, Doenitz was still getting virtually no support from the Luftwaffe. In desperation on December 14, Doenitz submitted a new request to the naval high command for the assignment of several squadrons of aircraft to the U-boat arm for combined operations.

Two weeks later, Doenitz met with Admiral Raeder and went into the matter in more detail. Raeder was sympathetic but did not want to quarrel with Goering, so he sent Doenitz to see General Jodl at OKW, which, theoretically at least, controlled all the armed services. Actually, all control rested in one man, Hitler. Raeder knew that, and he knew how to proceed. Jodl was sympathetic to Doenitz's request for at least the services of a dozen long-range Condor aircraft every day, and he took the matter up with Hitler, which was the only way it could be resolved because of Goering's special position in the government, as heir apparent to Hitler.

Hitler then arbitrarily ordered Air Group 40 to move under the Command of Admiral Doenitz, and then Goering came around in a hurry and assigned Lieutenant Colonel Herlinghausen to command of Group 40. Immediately Doenitz and Herlinghausen got to work on combined operations. At first there were two Condors available for flights over the areas west of Britain. Even so, it was difficult. The Condors had to fly from from French ports to the North Channel, and then cut back to the Norwegian coast because the distances were so great. This put them at the mercy of the ever changeable weather in Scandinavia.

In January 1941 Doenitz made two attempts to concentrate U-boats on convoys in connection with air reconnaissance, but there were not enough aircraft to do the job properly, and both attempts failed.

In fact, the potential of the air-sea search for convoys never was achieved in the North Atlantic, largely because of the failure of the Luftwaffe to produce long-range aircraft and assign enough of them to do the job.

The potential was more nearly realized in the South, from the Bay of Biscay bases, but even here in the winter of 1941, not much could be done because of the shortage of long-distance aircraft.

But the North Atlantic was the big problem. In the early months of 1941, Doenitz realized this and did what he could to increase the "eyes" available to him.

One hopeful development came in the summer of 1940, when the new ally, Italy, offered to put her one hundred U-boat fleet at the disposal of the Germans. Doenitz took no more than twenty-four hours to respond favorably, and a few days later, Admiral Parona, the Italian counterpart to Doenitz, came to see the German commander. They agreed that the overall control of activity in the Atlantic would be in the hands of the Germans, but that the Italian boats would operate under Italian command.

So that summer several Italian U-boat skippers were brought to Germany and sent out on operational patrols with the best German captains, to give the Italians a feel for the U-boat arm's methods of operation. A base for the Italians was then established at Bordeaux, and Admiral Parona sent Commander Sestini to join Doenitz's staff.

By the end of summer, twenty-seven Italian submarines had moved up to Bordeaux and the first Italian operations under German management were carried out in the area of the Azores. Doenitz allocated to the Italians the southern part of the North Atlantic, hoping thereby to increase his "eyes." But this did not work at all. In eight weeks of operations, the Italians did not once help the Germans out with information about convoys. Their reports were like those of the Luftwaffe; they came too late or they were inaccurate. What Doenitz learned was that the Italian method of submarine operations did not mesh with the German. The story of the Italian submarine *Durbo* gives an inkling of Doenitz's problem.

The *Durbo* was a 650-ton boat with two diesel and two electric engines. She carried six torpedo tubes, and a 3.9-inch gun on deck. She could travel sixty-seven hundred miles.

After the cooperative venture began, the *Durbo* was assigned to work off the Spanish coast against British convoys. She sailed on October 8. Her captain kept her on the surface at night and below in the daytime. He saw many British ships through his periscope, including a British destroyer on October 17. But he did not attack any of them. "It is better to destroy a few ships than to damage many," said her skipper. This was exactly the opposite philosophy to that of Doenitz, who believed in striking the enemy in any way possible. As Churchill knew so well, a damaged ship meant work in the shipyard, and delays in moving cargo, all essential matters in the war.

As of October 18, the skipper of the *Durbo* learned that his submarine had an oil leak. On the surface he put all available hands to work to stop it. When the daylight grew bright, he took the boat down to one hundred feet, but the leak had not stopped, although he thought it had.

The *Durbo* was still below the surface at 5:25 that evening when along came two British patrol planes, which spotted the trail of oil on the surface and bombed at the end of it. The *Durbo* went down to two hundred feet and then down to four hundred feet for safety's sake. At that depth the plates strained and the oil leak increased.

While the *Durbo* was still below, up came the British destroyers *Firedrake* and *Wrestler*, summoned by the patrol planes. The destroyers sighted the oil patches, and in a few minutes the asdic operator of the *Firedrake* had made contact with the submarine. Depth charges set at 350 feet produced a larger air bubble. The two destroyers dropped more depth charges, and in a few moments the submarine came popping to the surface. The *Wrestler* opened fire and the submarine dived. The destroyers dropped more depth charges and this time got more oil.

After fifty depth charges had been expended, the *Durbo* came up again, and both destroyers opened fire. One shell hit the conning tower. The crew began to abandon the submarine, and asked the destroyers to come alongside and take them off.

"Swim for it," said the hard-hearted British who were manning the ships' boats. A British sublieutenant boarded the submarine, and ordered an officer to go below with him to search for papers. The Italian officer did not want to go; he pulled away and jumped into the water. The British officer then went below and found many papers, but also saw that the submarine was settling and the water was rising in the control room. So he got out—and just in time, because the Italians had set scuttling charges, and just as the British boats pulled away from the submarine, the charges blew up and the submarine sank.

Aboard the *Wrestler*, the destroyer captain looked through the papers collected from the submarine, and found code books, and charts showing the operating area assigned to several Italian submarines by the Germans. Such loot would never have been found on a German U-boat; the discipline was too good for that. And so as the result of the sinking of the *Durbo*, at least one other Italian submarine was caught and sunk.

The whole affair was an Italian comic opera.

The Germans were not amused. Doenitz's staff worked up some statistics. The Italians had put in 243 days at sea in the joint operational area, and they sank one ship of 4,800 tons. Their potential was thus twenty tons of shipping per day at sea. In the same period the German submarines spent 378 days at sea and sank eighty ships, which amounted to 435,000 tons. The potential per sea day for the Germans was 1,115 tons.

After puzzling why the Italians should be so inferior to the German U-boat force, Doenitz reached some conclusions.

"The Italian submarine service had in peacetime been trained along the good old-fashioned lines, in accordance with which the submarine, acting independently, took up its position and waited for its target to appear, upon which it then delivered its attack submerged. The excellent gun armament carried by the Italian submarines was designed for the bombardment of enemy bases. They lacked the years of training in mobile warfare which the German U-boats had received. They were not masters of the arts of locating and reporting the presence of the enemy; nor of maintaining, unseen and for hours and sometimes for days on end, stubborn contact with him."

The Italian crews, to operate with the Germans, would have to be completely retrained, a matter that could not be accomplished in a few weeks, and one that Doenitz had no time to undertake. Further, the Italian U-boats were not designed to operate in the cold waters of the North Atlantic. The conning tower was long and high, and offered a conspicuous silhouette at all times when the boat was above water. Furthermore, the Italian submarines did not have a diesel air supply mast in the conning tower, which meant the hatch always had to be left open when running on the surface, to secure an adequate air supply for the diesel engines. In the North Atlantic this meant shipping a lot of water in bad weather when the waves broke over the conning tower.

Admiral Parona addressed himself to these problems. He sent the Italian crews to the Baltic to train with the Germans. He ordered the Italian boats scheduled for the North Atlantic to be modified. But it was not enough for Doenitz, who had too many problems of his own. So the cooperative venture came to an end that fall. The Italians took up positions in the west and south of the German operational area. And there they achieved many successes, doing things in their own way under their own command.

It was only with the greatest reluctance that Admiral Doenitz gave up on his Italian allies, because his U-boat situation grew more serious every day that winter of 1940–41. The total number of U-boats decreased so that sometimes only eighteen were operational at a time. Of these, only a third might be in contact with the British, and at one point for several days, only three boats were in contact.

When this period came, Doenitz finally swallowed his revulsion against a mixed force and ordered the Italian boats, which had been doing so well in the southern sector, to come up north and operate south of Iceland, to help the German boats in the war against the convoys.

Again, the experiment was a failure, because the Italians simply would not stick to a situation long enough to give Doenitz the convoy information he needed. The Italians did sink some ships, but they did not operate as a wolf pack, and so on May 5, Doenitz finally concluded a new agreement with Admiral Parona, splitting the Atlantic, with the Italians to operate west of Gibraltar and in a small area of the North Atlantic south of the main convoy routes, and in the area off Freetown, Africa. Later on the Italians would move into the South Atlantic off

Brazil, and there would achieve some spectacular successes.

Doenitz wished them all well. But his overweening concern was the North Atlantic, for he knew very well that the U-boat war would succeed or fail on the major routes from North America to Britain. Here was Britain's major lifeline. Here the war could be won.

Admiral Raeder's staff was forever pushing Doenitz to extend his sphere of operations, a plan the admiral resisted as well as he could, because it could only dilute the strength of his battle force. There were plenty of ships to be sunk in the North Atlantic. The problem was finding them, and this would be done by more, not fewer, U-boats in the area.

In the winter of 1940–41, the U-boats were hampered by the worst weather that had struck the North Atlantic in several years. But Doenitz sent them out anyhow, to search, search. And they did.

They were looking for the convoys.

Convoy HX90 set out from Canada bound for Liverpool. The time was the end of November. Because the Irish refused to give Britain bases on Irish soil, the convoy would have to steam far north, through the harsh weather, and down through the Northern Approaches. The British had already learned that the occupation of France had made the Southern Approaches too dangerous.

HX90 consisted of forty-one ships when the convoy set out, but two had suffered mechanical failures and had turned back to North America. Nine ships had been separated in the stormy weather that blew from November 24 to November 28, so the convoy was reorganized at sea into nine columns of thirty ships.

On December 1 the convoy picked up one of the old four-stack American destroyers, now British. The convoy also picked up a U-boat, *U–101*, which it did not know about. As soon as the skipper of *U–101* made contact, he radioed Admiral Doenitz, who called in his wolf pack. Shortly afterwards, Prien's *U–47*, Kretschmer's *U–99* and Lieutenant Otto Salman's *U–452* were on the way to intercept the convoy before it could reach the Western Approaches to Britain, and powerful air and sea escort.

That night at 8:14 the *U–101* torpedoed the ship *Appalachee* on the outside starboard column, and then the *Loch Ranza*. The first ship sank, but the second kept going, after picking up the survivors of the *Appalachee*. The explosions were reported to the convoy commander, who was having his dinner. He went to the bridge of his ship *Botavon*, but on the bridge he saw only some lights to starboard and no signals, so he went back to his dinner. A couple of ships had somehow got tangled up, he decided.

At 1:00 A.M. the convoy altered course, heading for the point of rendezvous with the escorts that would take them into English waters. So did the U-boats. Half an hour later, the ship *Ville d'Arlon* dropped out of her column, afflicted with difficulties. Lieutenant Commander Prien watched her come and then torpedoed her. An hour later the *U–101* torpedoed the *Lady Glanely*, the lead ship in the outside port column.

Prien now surfaced and moved up to the convoy. He came right to the edge, and the men of the tanker *Conch* on the bridge saw the submarine on the surface as it torpedoed them. The *Conch* fell out of line.

Prien then moved in on the *Dunsley*, the next ship in the column, and opened fire with his deck gun. The merchant ship started firing back, and peppered the water around the U-boat. Prien fired ten more rounds, and his gun was an eighty-eight-millimeter, so they did plenty of damage when they hit. The freighter fired star shells, and Prien did not like that, so he moved away.

The convoy made an emergency turn, and then resumed its base course. The U-boats were still out there, trailing and waiting, like foxes after sheep.

The most spectacular sight of the night was the torpedoing of the ammunition ship *Kavak*, the end vessel in the starboard outside column, by the *U–101*. She blew up with a flash of light that made the sky seem like midday.

The U-boats continued to attack; *U–52* torpedoed the steamer *Tasso*, which had lagged behind, and then the steamer *Goodleigh*. The *Goodleigh* got three torpedoes from three U-boats. That was the end of it for the moment, and the British believed wrongly that the end had come because they were nearing the Western Approaches and more escort vessels. The real reason was that Prien's *U–47* had run out of torpedoes, Mengerson's *U–101* was having trouble with one diesel engine, and Kretschmer's *U–99* had turned away to stalk HMS *Forfar*, a sixteen-thousand-ton armed merchant cruiser.

Convoy HX90 had been assaulted by the U-boats beginning at fifty-four degrees north and twenty degrees west, and now had reached fifty-six degrees north and seventeen degrees west, which was the point where she was supposed to pick up the escort vessels that would see her safely into port. Those escorts, the destroyers *Viscount*, *Vanquisher*, and *Gentian*, on the previous evening had just left convoy OB251, bound for the west to pick up war goods, and were searching for the new convoy to take home. OB251 had dispersed, because there were no escorts to take her across the broad Atlantic, and besides, the Germans were not yet operating in mid-Atlantic. But just now the dispersal meant there were a number of ships in this area, and a number of U-boats attracted by HX90. Doenitz had called in *U–43*, *U–95*, *U–94*, and *U–140* after the first wolf pack had begun to run out of torpedoes.

These U-boats crisscrossed the area, seeking individual ships and stragglers from the convoy. In short order they sank two freighters and a tanker. A few hours later came the word to Doenitz: Kretschmer had found the armed cruiser *Forfar* and sunk her, and also three more ships had been sunk. Also the tanker *Conch*, which had been torpedoed by Prien's *U–47*, was torpedoed again on December 2 by the *U–95*—three times—but still managed to keep afloat until that evening, when she was torpedoed by Kretschmer for the fifth time, and sank.

The escort vessels, which had hoped to take HX90 home safely, got so involved in answering distress calls and picking up survivors from the sinking ships that they were totally disorganized, and so HX90 had no protection. The convoy was found by the *U–94*, which began torpedoing ships like a hunter popping at a whole herd of deer.

Then that day the Focke-Wulff Condor assigned to the U-boat cooperative venture found the convoy and began bombing. One escort came up and engaged the Condor, and ultimately it flew away. So finally HX90, still without escort, or at least properly organized escort, managed to limp into port. Of the forty-one ships that had set out from America, only twenty arrived.

The fate of HX90 created a stir at the Admiralty, and Churchill demanded that something drastic had to be done. The answer was more escort, and now that the threat of the invasion of Britain was over, the escorts could be provided. The decision was made to take the ships farther west under escort before leaving them, and thus to pick up the homeward-bound convoys sooner with their precious goods. When the sinking figures for December 1940 were added up, it was found that they were high, but largely because of the fate of convoy HX90. The changes of routing, the increase of escort, and the increased activity of the RAF all helped to bring the sinkings down to 127,000 tons in January. The bad weather helped; so did a change in the merchant codes, which stopped Doenitz from reading the British mail. So did the installation of radar on escort vessels, making it possible to detect submarines on the surface. So did another development, the Leigh light. This was an adaptation of a tank's battle searchlight to aircraft. When installed on a plane and turned on suddenly on the deck of a surfaced submarine, it blinded the crew and illuminated the U-boat for an attack.

And still other developments were coming to fruition. The United States was getting ready to send a number of B-24 bombers to Britain, and they would be found admirable for long-range search and bombing of U-boats. Ninety trawlers converted to become escort vessels had been delivered to the Royal Navy, and the *Flower*-class corvettes designed and ordered in 1939 specifically to fight U-boats were beginning to come off the ways in Britain.

There were bad times to come, to be sure, but Britain was building her sea defenses.

CHAPTER 15

After the Fall

The British had cast their lot firmly with General de Gaulle's Free French in the agreement signed between De Gaulle and Prime Minister Churchill in August 1940. The disaster at Dakar really made no difference, although it did show how little capital De Gaulle had in his homeland at the time. In London, too, there were many doubters. "The greatest cross I have to bear is the Cross of Lorraine," Churchill himself is reported to have said, referring to the symbol De Gaulle had chosen for his movement.

In West Africa early in November, the Free French gained a little when Colonel Leclerc led a force of Free French volunteers to attack Libreville in French Equatorial Africa. In a week's time Leclerc captured Libreville, and the Free French had their first piece of territory, but it was woefully inadequate to give them a real claim to greatness.

In France, in London, everywhere, almost all the French were Pétainist in sympathy. De Gaulle tried to raise volunteers, but at the end of three months, had only about three thousand adherents.

Yet Churchill never wavered. He needed a symbol of French resistance, and De Gaulle was the best he could get. "I never ceased to feel a unity with France," he said. "People who have not been subjected to the personal stresses which fell upon prominent Frenchmen in the awful ruin of their country should be careful in their judgements of individuals. His feeling for France . . . I felt sure that the French nation would do its best for the common cause according to the facts presented to it. When they were told that their only salvation lay in following the advice of the illustrious Marshal Pétain, and that England, which had given them so little help, would soon be conquered or give in, very little choice was offered to the masses. But I was sure they wanted us to win, and nothing would give them more joy than to see us continue the struggle with vigor.''

Diplomatic relations with Vichy had been broken in June, but Churchill managed to keep in touch with France, and French affairs, through contacts with America and Canada. America had sent Admiral William Leahy as ambassador to Vichy, and Canada had Minister Pierre Dupuis there, so Britain had its window on France. Sub rosa Churchill continued to deal with Pétain's representatives, although in full knowledge that this pained General de Gaulle.

On October 21 Churchill used the BBC to make a broadcast to the French people, which he delivered with a flourish during a German air raid. He promised the French that Britain would fight on, that she was winning the air battle of Britain, and that Hitler had the foulest of designs on France. Ultimately he warned, ''All Europe, if he has his way, will be reduced to one uniform Bocheland, to be exploited, pillaged, and bullied by his Nazi gangsters. You will excuse my speaking frankly because this is not a time to mince words. It is not defeat that France will now be made to suffer at German hands, but the doom of complete obliteration.''

Hitler had been persuaded by Admiral Raeder that if Britain could not be invaded, she could still be defeated, and that the proper cockpit for the struggle was the Mediterranean. So two days after Churchill's address to the French people, Hitler traveled to the French-Spanish border town of Hendaye to meet Generalissimo Franco, who had indicated that he might join the war against Britain if the stakes were high enough. He wanted a large chunk of the French colonies, and Gibraltar.

The meeting was not a success from Hitler's point of view, because the British had shown so much resiliency, withstanding the Italian attacks in the Mediterranean while fending of the German air attack on England.

And in France, as well, the reputation of Britain rebounded in the autumn of 1940.

Sisley Huddleston, erstwhile correspondent of the London *Times* in France, and Briton born but Frenchman by inclination and naturalization, had moved from Paris to Monaco after the French surrender to escape the zone of France occupied by the Germans. From there he continued to observe and sometimes to report on events in France.

Many Frenchmen held a deep resentment—hatred—for "le Boche," their traditional enemy, but in the first months of the Vichy government, there was no overt resistance movement. There was no plan, there was no organization. Huddleston was aware of a gathering feeling of resistance. The most important aspect of it in that time was the legion of former combatants, old soldiers, who supported Pétain and were sure that ultimately he would rid himself of the Germans.

On the same day that Hitler met with Franco at Hendaye, Churchill was meeting with Professor Louis Rougier in London. The professor was the representative of Marshal Pétain. British and French representatives had first met in Madrid and talked about the possibility of an accord. Then Pétain had met Professor Rougier through a mutual friend, and had entrusted him with the mission. The secret meeting almost failed before it began. A false report in an American newspaper had said that France and Germany had concluded a separate peace in which

France had given Alsace-Lorraine to Germany, and Nice to Italy. Churchill, who had just learned of the report, was furious, but ultimately he calmed down and learned the truth, that there was no such agreement.

So Professor Rougier and Prime Minister Churchill made an agreement. The British would help the French in all the ways they could if the French would maintain passive resistance to the Germans.

The British had been blockading the French coast, stopping vessels bound for France and searching for contraband war materials. Now Churchill agreed to lift most of the blockade, to permit vessels from French ports in North and West Africa to bring food into unoccupied France. Churchill also agreed to stop the British personal attacks on Marshal Pétain. In return the French agreed not to surrender their fleet to the Germans, no matter how much pressure was put on, to retain all French ports in North Africa, and ultimately to reenter the war on the Allied side "whenever it can strike effectively."

Resistance in France had to move slowly. In occupied France the Germans and pro-German Frenchmen were in control. The national newspapers, the *journaux d'information*, had almost all remained in Paris and were full of German propaganda. The Germans also subsidized newspapers.

The *journaux d'opinion*, for the most part, moved out of Paris into unoccupied France. They faced censorship but could, if with restraint, publish fairly freely. But they could not fulminate against the government or the Germans. The Communists, who would play so great a role in the resistance of the future, were just now on the German side, since the USSR was linked with Hitler by the pact of 1939. So the Communists took a line close to that of the Nazis. Jews began to be mistreated. First the Jews were forced to register in the fall of 1940, and then on October 18, a new Vichy law barred Jews from public service jobs and key positions in industry and the media.

The end of 1940 saw France divided into two camps, geographically, but even more so and in a different delineation, morally. It could be suicidal to alienate the Germans openly, and at this stage there was nothing to be gained by it. But there were two courses of conduct open to all:

One was to remain in France and stand up to the Germans. One could negotiate, even temporize, in behalf of the French people, and that is what Pétain did.

The second course was to really show zeal in the service of the enemy, and that attitude characterized Pierre Laval.

Marshal Pétain recognized Laval's toadyism to the enemy from the beginning and confided to intimates that he wished to rid himself of Laval. In the meeting with Hitler at Montoire, Pétain had played a waiting game, listening to Hitler's request for French participation on Germany's side in the war against Britain, but carefully not acceding. Indeed, at the time, Pétain was in contact with Churchill, and the agreement between them was being worked out. But Laval took the position that Pétain had promised truly to cooperate with Hitler, and he spread that story around Vichy. That is when Marshal Pétain decided that Laval would have to go.

Laval offered to negotiate with the Germans over many delicate points. One was the return of French war prisoners, many of whom had been shipped to Germany as slave labor. One was the return of several French departments, which had been placed by the Germans for administration under the Belgian government. (What difference did it make to the Germans which of their slave states had control?)

Another question was the fate of Alsace-Lorraine, which the Germans wanted to annex. Still another was the enormous indemnity assessed by the Germans, of four hundred million francs per day. A final point was the desire of the Vichy government for freer communications with occupied France.

Yes, Laval set about negotiating these questions, but he gave Pétain and others the feeling that he represented the German point of view and not the French.

The break came over a peculiarly Gallic issue. The Duke of Reichstadt, also known as the King of Rome, the son of Napoleon, had been buried in Vienna when he died. Laval proposed that the ashes of the duke be brought from Vienna to Paris and interred with the remains of his father in the tomb of the Invalides. It was the sort of theatrical gesture that so appealed to Hitler, and he embraced it. It would be accomplished at night, and on hand would be Marshal Pétain and Adolf Hitler, who would grasp hands as the coffin was lowered into the tomb. This act would symbolize the reconciliation of Germany and France, and the two nations would go on to prosecute the war against Britain.

Pétain's friends convinced him—whether it was true or not—that Laval was leading a plot to involve the marshal in this "removal of the remains" in order to commit France irrevocably to the Hitler policies, and that the marshal would be detained at Versailles while a new government headed by Laval and others known to be pro-German was set up in Paris.

At that point Pétain said that Laval had to go. He was prepared to defy the Germans, and run the risk of Hitler declaring a general government of the sort set up in Poland. He was prepared to sacrifice himself if need be, but he would not go along with the Boche.

So, on the eve of the ceremony at Les Invalides, Marshal Pétain mustered his indignation and demanded the resignation of the ministers of the government. When he had all of them, he announced that he was accepting only two, the resignations of Laval and Minister Ripert, of Education. Laval protested. Pétain said coldly that Laval had been keeping him in the dark while negotiating with the Germans. Laval warned that what the marshal was doing was irrevocable and would show him to be the enemy of the Germans. Pétain was immovable. Laval left.

And on the night of the great ceremony, Pétain did not show up, so there was no ceremony and no wedding of France and Germany at the Napoleonic tomb.

Vichy went into a state of siege. Trains did not run. Laval was arrested and confined to his house. Some advocated a quick midnight trial and then a firing squad. But a few days later, Otto Abetz, the German ambassador, arrived with an armed escort to demand in Hitler's name the freeing of Laval, and it was done. But Pétain would not have Laval back in the cabinet, and the Germans did not insist. Pétain had defied Hitler in his own way, and he had succeeded. Hitler was still hoping for reconciliation with France, and so delayed the harshness. No gauleiter was appointed to rule France with an iron hand. Pétain was retained in position, but Admiral Darlan, who was regarded by the Germans as more politically reliable than the old marshal, was thrust upon him by the Germans as prime minister.

At this stage of the war, the French were beginning to move in Africa. Many of the "legion" were going there, and the Americans were sending many representatives to French North Africa, many more than were strictly needed to manage trade and other commercial relations.

There in North Africa, General Weygand was supervising the organization of a new French army, with the full consent of Marshal Pétain. The army was waiting, and on the horizon was already the plan for the Allied invasion of North Africa, at which time the army would be expected (by Churchill and by the Americans) to make its move to fight the Germans.

In these early days of occupation and nonoccupation,

of the pretense that the French would be allowed to make their own way, the Germans did not interfere much in the free zone. Sisley Huddleston, who traveled up from his new home in Monaco on some business, found that people in the cafés and hotels talked openly of current affairs and were as outspoken as they wished in their views. Some advocated resistance against the Germans. Some advocated passivity. All seemed eager to tell their views. Huddleston was only in Vichy for a few hours before he learned that some of the most important civil servants were meeting regularly with members of resistance units, and that most of the government knew precisely what was going on. He met people who spoke to him longingly of the day when the British and Americans would land in France. "We have had enough of the Boche," one of them said.

Vichy was a strange dislocated place, where Frenchmen pretended they were free but knew in their hearts that any false step would be met with German strength. It was as it had been with the arrest of Laval; the Germans made sure nothing upset their plans. As long as the French did not openly defy them, matters could stand as they were. But the French knew. There was no freedom even in Vichy. They had become a part of the Greater German Reich, willy-nilly. As observer, Huddleston said:

"Vichy could not last. It had no dynamic essence. Its function was negative, not positive. It was tolerated. It lived on sufferance. The marshal was too old, too much the prey of contending forces, to continue to give the necessary impulsion; he was overwhelmed by his own ministers."

Thus the Vichy government would fall into the hands of Laval and his friends, and as affairs worsened in France, would ultimately fall to the Germans. But at that moment Vichy was free France, where the tricoleur still flew. Here is Sisley Huddleston's recollection of that time:

"I went with M. to witness the trouping of the colors. It was Sunday morning, before the Hotel du Parc was a crowd of Vichy residents. The guard, with white gauntlets, in leather tunics, took up its post. Military music rang out in the clear air. At a signal, we all uncovered, and as we stood at attention the flag of France was hauled up the mast. The Marshal came out on the balcony to salute the tricoleur. It was, for me, an unforgettable moment. France was invaded . . . but there remained one little corner where the French flag flew, and while it flew all was not lost. Purely symbolic? But certain symbols are woven into our lives. In that flag, now flapping and streaming in the wind, was a promise of deliverance. Conscious as I was of the unhappy condition of the land I loved, I saw in the flag a pledge and a token of the imperishable France. The flag sent out its message of freedom. France was not wholly submerged, was not without hope. France lived, since the flag, bright in the morning sunshine, triumphant in the wind of springtime, waved like a living thing."

France remained, and in the early spring of 1941, the war swirled around her in the water and the air of the North, and on water, land, and air in the South. For the moment, France was quiescent, waiting.

294   THE FALL OF FRANCE

book. There a letter had the tone of a recollection of that time.

NOTES

1 The Way to Dunkirk

A basic source for this chapter was Heinz Guderian's *Panzer Leader*. Corelli Barnett's *Desert Generals* was also useful. Flower and Reeves's *The Taste of Courage* was useful for looks at the German and British sides. The most reliable source for the story of why Hitler stopped the panzers is Keitel, who was involved all the way. Hayward's *Dunkirk* was vital to the re-creation of the atmosphere in that French port city during the BEF evacuation. Churchill's *Their Finest Hour* gave the high-level views, and Huddleston's *France* showed the French situation and feeling. Guderian's order to his panzers is from his book. Somerville's chronology of World War II was helpful in keeping track of events in their time frame.

2 In Dunkirk Harbor

Hayward's book was vital to this chapter, as was Guderian's. Nieh's book on the Luftwaffe gave some detail about the German air force activity, as did the Fraenkel biography of Marshal Goering. Montgomery's *Memoirs* give an assessment of Lord Gort.

3 Tragedy Called Triumph

The Luftwaffe book was useful here, and so was Hayward. The story of the high-level German machinations comes from the Keitel memoirs and from Shirer's two books, *The Rise and Fall of the Third Reich* and *The Collapse of the Third Republic*. Hayward is particularly harsh on the RAF failures at Dunkirk. The quotation of Churchill is from *Their Finest Hour*.

4 The Fall of France

The political material about French events is from Shirer's *Collapse of the Third Republic*, that about Britain from Churchill. Von Rundstedt's quotation is from the Flower book. The Guderian story is from his book. The stories of the meetings of French and British are from Shirer, Churchill, and Huddleston.

5 The Last Days of French Independence

The story of the last days of French independence comes from Shirer, Huddleston, and Churchill. Guderian's book details the advance of the German troops through France. The story of French-British relations is from Shirer and Churchill. Keitel provided the glimpse of Hitler's plans. The machinations at Vichy are detailed in Shirer.

6 Armistice

The story of the signing of the armistice comes from the two Shirer books and from Keitel. The story of the French army is from Huddleston. The material about De Gaulle is from Churchill. The material about Laval is from Huddleston and Shirer.

7 The Fate of the Fleet; the Fate of France

The story of the fate of the French fleet comes from Churchill and from materials from the Admiralty files of the British Office of Public Records in Kew. The material about Laval and Vichy comes from Shirer and Huddleston.

8   Operation Sea Lion

The material about Operation Sea Lion is from Churchill, Somerville, Shirer's book on the Nazis, Doenitz's memoirs and the Keitel memoirs, and Von der Porten. The Hitler order is from Keitel. The material about the Battle of Britain is from the Goering biography and the Luftwaffe book. Bekker was also useful here.

9   Britain Strikes Back

The Farago book was important to this chapter, and so was the Stevenson book. But most important was Nigel West's *MI5*.

10   Britain at Bay

This chapter depended on the Churchill story of Britain at bay, but even more on Dr. Jones's *The Wizard War*. The quotations from the German newspapers are from Shirer, as is the reference to Count Ciano. The beginning of the Blitz was noted by Keitel, and by the Goering biographers and in the Luftwaffe book, as well as by Churchill.

11   The German Dilemma

This chapter depended on research for my *Hitler's War*, published by McGraw Hill in 1988, and the Churchill book for the material on Hitler and Lend-Lease. I used the Shirer book on the Third Reich for the material on Poland, and the Goering biography for the story of Goering's art looting. *The Desert Generals* was used in telling the story of the Italian campaign in Africa. The story of the incident at Dakar is from Churchill and Shirer. The Montroire affair is thoroughly explored in Huddleston, who knew Pétain better than any other Englishman.

12   The War Shifts South

The Desert Generals was a basic source for this chapter, and the Churchill book was useful. The source for the material about the Eden mission is Churchill. The material about Hitler and his staff is from Shirer and Keitel.

13   The Battle of the Atlantic Begins

This chapter depended heavily on research materials from the Office of Public Records in London, particularly on the papers on antisubmarine warfare, and on the Doenitz memoirs. Von der Porten was also useful, as well as Withers. The Kretschmer story is from the official German U-boat records, in the Withers book.

14   Struggle at Sea

Morison's *Battle of the Atlantic* was important in this chapter, as was the Churchill book and Von der Porten. The Doenitz memoirs were also valuable, and the Withers compilation. The story of the Italian submarines in action is from research in the Admiralty files at the British Office of Public Records.

15   After the Fall

The Churchill book, Shirer's book on France, and Huddleston were all important in the formation of this chapter.

BIBLIOGRAPHY

Barnett, Corelli. *The Desert Generals*. New York: Berkley, 1960.

Bekker, C. D. *Defeat at Sea*. New York: Henry Holt, 1955.

Churchill, Winston. *Their Finest Hour*. Boston: Houghton Mifflin, 1949.

Doenitz, Karl. *Memoirs*. New York: Belmont Books, 1965.

Farago, Ladislas. *The Game of the Foxes*. New York: David McKay, 1971.

Flower, Desmond, and James Reeves, eds. *The Taste of Courage*. Vol. 1. New York: Berkley, 1960.

Fraenkel, Heinrich, and Roger Manvel. *Hermann Goering*. Herrsching: Manfred Pawlak Verlagsgesellschaft, Germany, 1962.

Gorlitz, Walter. *The Memoirs of Field Marshal Keitel*. New York: Stein and Day, 1966.

Guderian, Heinz. *Panzer Leader*. New York: E. P. Dutton, 1957.

Hayward, Nicholas. *Dunkirk, the Patriotic Myth*. New York: Simon and Schuster, 1980.

Huddleston, Sisley. *France, the Tragic Years*. Boston: Western Islands, 1965.

Jones, R. V. *The Wizard War*. New York: Coward McCarm; Groghoyen, 1978.

Montgomery, Bernard L. *Memoirs*. New York: Signet Books, 1958.

Morison, Samuel Eliot. *The Battle of the Atlantic*. Bortani: Atlantic Little Brown, 1956.

Nieh, L. D. *Die Luftwaffe. 1918–45*. Vienna: Paul Neff Verlag, 1973.

Overy, R. J. *The Air War 1939–45*. New York: Stein and Day, 1983.

Shirer, William L. *The Rise and Fall of the Third Reich*. New York: Simon and Schuster, 1960.

———. *The Collapse of the Third Republic*. New York: Simon and Schuster, 1960.

Somerville, Donald. *World War II Day by Day*. Greenwich, Conn.: Dorset Press, 1989.

Stevenson, William. *A Man Called Intrepid*. New York: Harcourt, Brace, Jovanovich, 1976.

Von der Porten, Edward. *The German Navy in World War II*. New York: T. Y. Cowell Co., 1966.

West, Nigel. *MI5*. New York: Stein and Day, 1962.

Withers, Andrew J., RN. *The U-Boat War in the Atlantic, German Naval History*. Facsimile edition from the German naval records. London: Her Majesty's Stationery Office, 1989.

INDEX

Abeta, Otto, 202
Aboukir, 17
Abrial, Admiral, 24
Abwehr (German intelligence agency), 93, 108, 114–118
Aircraft production: Britain, 94; Germany, 94–95
Alexander, H.R.L.G., 29, 32, 35
Alfieri, Dino, 85
Algeria, 43, 73
Alibert, Raphael, 58–59, 77
Alsace-Lorraine, 198, 200
Apollo, 169
Appalachee, 192
Arandora Star, 109
Argus, 149
Ark Royal, 76, 148
Armistice: of 1918: *See* World War I; of 1940: *See* Franco-German armistice; Franco-Italian armistice.
Atlantic, Battle of, 162–179, 181
Atlantic Fleet (U.S.), 181
Auriol, Vincent, 77
Austen, Godwin, 146
Australia, 120, 143

Babini, General, 157
Badoglio, Marshal, 138
Balbo, Marshal, 144
Barham, 137
Barratt, Air Vice Marshal, 45
Basilisk, 31
Battle of Atlantic, 162–179, 181
Battle of Britain, 107, 136, 185
Baudouin, Paul, 52–53, 57–59, 68, 72, 77, 78
B-24 bombers, 195
Beaufighters, 128
BEF: *See* British Expeditionary Force.
Belgium, 10, 12–13, 32, 83, 133, 140; collapse of Belgian army, 13; Fifth Column activity, 109–111; unconditional surrender to German army, 13, 18
Ben-my-Chree, 32
Bergonzoli, General, 154; capture of, 160
Biddle, Anthony J. Drexel, 49, 52
Billotte, General, 7; death of, 7
Bismarck, 96

211

Black Watch Regiment (Britain), 146
Blanchard, General, 7
Bleichrodt, Heinrich, 173
Blenheim bombers, 30, 128, 151
Blitz, the, 126–128, 185
Bock, General von, 10, 41
Botavan, 192
Brak, Jan Willen Ter, 117–118; suicide by, 118
Brauchitsch, Walther von, 2, 63, 64, 88, 132, 152
Brazza, 163
Bretagne, 76
Britain, Battle of, 107, 136, 185
British Expeditionary Force (BEF), 2, 28, 37, 38, 97, 107; evacuation from Dunkirk, 3–6, 11–14, 17, 25, 28–29, 34–36
Brooke, Alan, 18
Bulgaria, 152
Bullitt, William, 37, 38–39, 70; Reynaud, meeting with, 39

Calypso, 135
Campbell, Ronald, 55, 67–68, 72
Canada, 4, 165, 197
Canaris, Admiral, 114, 118
Canary Islands, 142, 153
Cape Verde Islands, 142, 153
Caroli, Gosta, 117
Chamberlain, Neville, 151
Charly, Lieutenant Colonel, 61; death of, 61
Chautemps, Camille, 58
Chiang Kai-shek, 120
Churchill, Winston, 3, 5, 24, 29, 31–32, 35–36, 38–39, 44–46, 48–52, 55, 67, 68, 71–72, 73, 74, 76, 81–87, 89, 96–100, 103, 107, 109, 110, 112, 119–123, 126, 128, 130–131, 136–138, 145–151, 155, 160–161, 164, 173, 179–184, 187, 196–199; agreement with Reynaud on declaration of union with France and Britain, 50; demanding help for France, 38; meeting with Reynaud, 5–6; plans to put De Gaulle in power at Dakar, 136–137
Ciano, Galeazzo, 114, 126
Clintonia, 178
Clouston, J. C., 16
Coldstream Guards (Britain), 33, 153
Collegian, 172
Comfort, 20
Conch, 192, 193–194
Condor aircraft, 185
Convoy HX71, 170
Convoy HX72, 170, 172
Convoy HX79, 178
Convoy HX84, 182
Convoy HX90, 191, 193, 194
Convoy OA207, 167
Convoy OB216, 170
Convoy SC2, 167, 169, 170
Convoy SC3, 169
Convoy SC6, 173
Convoy SC7, 173
Creagh, Michael, 159
Crete, 151, 152
Cumberland, 137
Cunningham, Andrew, 54, 73, 74, 148–149, 150, 151
Czechoslovakia, 57, 130

Dakar, 136–137, 196

Dalton, Hugh, 82

Dandolo, 166–167

Darlan, Admiral, 54, 58, 67, 74, 75, 202; calling for war against Britain, 77

Davies, E. L., 21

de Gaulle, Charles, 40, 42–43, 44, 50, 51, 55–56, 66, 68–69, 74, 136–137, 150, 196; court-martial and sentence in absentia to death for desertion, 56, 66; fleeing to London, 51; Pétain's opinion of, 40; plans for taking over Dakar, 136–137; Weygand's opinion of, 40

Dietrich, Sepp, 8

Dill, John, 3, 44

Doenitz, Karl, 95, 139, 162–163, 164–175, 183, 184–194

Dunkirk, 1–36, 39–40, 67, 105; bombing of, 10; British Expeditionary Force, evacuation of, 3–6, 11–14, 17, 25, 29, 34–36; French troops, evacuation of, 28–29, 34–36; harbor at, 15–25; Luftwaffe's destruction of port facilities at, 2, 6–7, 10; surrender to Germans, 36–37

Dunquerque, 73, 75, 76

Dunsley, 192

Dunster Grange, 163

Dupuis, Pierre, 197

Durbo, 187–188

East Lancashire Regiment (Britain), 33

Eden, Anthony, 38, 44, 149

Egypt, 143–153

Eleventh Hussars (Britain), 144, 159

Erik Frisell, 163

Ervine-Andrews, Captain, 33

Esk, 32

Ethiopia, 135, 143

Fagalde, General, 12

Fifteenth Panzer Corps (Germany), 41

Fifth Column activity: Britain, 109–110, 112; France, 109–110; Holland, 109–110

Fifty-second Division (Britain), 38

Firedrake, 188

First Army (France), 9–10, 31; surrender to Germans, 40

First Infantry Division (Canada), 4, 38

First Panzer Division (Germany), 46, 51

Foch, Marshal, 62

Forbes, Admiral, 166

Force H (Britain), 73–74, 148, 149

Foudroyant, 31

Fourth Armored Division (France), 40

Foxhound, 74

Franco, Francisco, 139–140, 153, 198; meeting with Hitler, 139–140

Franco-German armistice (1940), 60–71

Franco-Italian armistice (1940), 69, 135, 141

Frank, Hans, 132

French fleet, 65, 67, 69, 72–80

Fricke, Kurt, 83

Funck, Freiherr von, 139

Gamelin, Maurice, 12, 97
Gensoul, Admiral, 74–76
Gentian, 193
Georges, Alophonse, 53
George VI, King of England, 151
Gibraltar, 138, 139–140, 141, 152
Gipsy King, 17–18
Gneisenau, 73, 96
Godfroy, Rene, 74
Goebbels, Joseph, 66, 125, 166
Goering, Hermann, 2–3, 14–15, 17, 63, 82, 86, 87, 92, 94, 102, 104, 123, 125, 126–127, 133, 185
Goodleigh, 193
Gort, Lord, 4–6, 7, 11–13, 24–25, 28, 29, 38
Gracie Fields, 23
Graf Spee, 96
Grafton, 20
Graziani, Rodolfo, 135, 138, 151, 152, 158
Greece, 141, 150–153, 155, 160–161; calling on Britain to honor commitment to fight Italian invasion, 150–151
Grenada, 21
Grenadier Guards (Britain), 32
Greyhound, 21–22
Gro, 168
Gross Deutschland Regiment (Germany), 9
Gubbins, Colin McV., 110
Guderian, Heinz, 1, 3, 8–9, 18, 22, 34, 40, 42, 46, 51–52, 64

Halder, Franz, 2, 84, 89, 132, 152

Herlinghausen, Lieutenant Colonel, 185
Hess, Rudolph, 63
Heydrich, Reinhard, 132
Himmler, Heinrich, 131–132
Hipper, 182
Hitler, Adolf, 1–3, 7–8, 9, 24, 30, 38–40, 43–44, 51, 60–65, 68, 70–71, 73, 75, 78, 82–94, 100–102, 103–106, 107, 111, 125, 126–128, 130–133, 135, 137–142, 143, 152–153, 155, 165, 185, 197–198, 199; calling off bombing of Britain, 106; Franco, meeting with, 139–140; issuing directive for conduct of air and naval war against England, 8, 82–94, 92–93; Mussolini, meeting with, 56–57, 141
HMS *Forfar,* 193
HMS *Keith,* 30
Holland, Cedric Swinton, 74, 75–76, 130, 133
Home Guardsmen (Britain), 102–103, 113–114
Hood, 76, 148
Hopkins, Harry, 180
Hotspur, 136
Huddleston, Sisley, 134, 140–141, 198, 203–204
Hull, Cordell, 39
Huntzinger, Charles, 57, 60, 62, 64–65, 67, 69, 75
Hurricane fighter planes, 30, 44, 149

Iceland, 165
Illustrious, 150, 151
India, 145
Ioanna, 163

Iron Duke, 107
Ironside, Edmund, 4, 109
Ismay, General, 44, 97
Italy, 43, 45, 69, 120, 138

Jackson, William, 111
Japan, 54, 86, 103, 120
Jervis Bay, 182
Jeschonnek, Hans, 88–89, 94
Jodl, General, 2, 64, 82, 87, 90, 152
Jones, R. V., 121–122
Jose de Larinaga, 168
Joubert, Philip, 121–122
Joyce, William, 113
JU 52 aircraft, 6
Julien, 163

Kavak, 192
Keitel, Wilhelm, 2, 56–57, 63, 64–67, 68, 84, 90, 93, 101, 130–131, 138, 139, 152
Kell, Vernon, 111
Kennedy, Joseph, 112
Kent, Tyler, 112–113, 130
Kenya, 135, 143, 145, 147
Keuchler, Georg von, 131
Keyes, Roger, 82, 119
King, Ernest J., 181
King, Mackenzie, 39
Kleist, General von, 1–3, 51
Knapp, Commander, 170–172
Knickebein beam, 123–124
Knox, Frank, 131
Kretschmer, Otto, 172, 175–178, 193–194
Kyma, 163

Lady Glanely, 192
Laval, Pierre, 49, 69–71, 76–79, 200–203; proposal to make Pétain dictator, 78
Leahy, William, 197
Le Brun, Albert, 50, 58–59, 68, 70, 80
Leclerc, Colonel, 196
Leeb, Ritter von, 52
Leigh light, 194
Lemnos Islands, 152
Libya, 154
Liebstandarte Division (Germany), 8, 9
Lindemann, Frederick, 119, 121–122
Lloyd, Lord, 55
Loch Ranza, 192
Lowestoff, 167, 168, 170
Luftwaffe, 7, 11, 20, 22, 31, 33–34, 40, 83, 94, 98, 102, 106; port facilities at Dunkirk, destruction of, 2, 6–7, 10; Royal Air Force's failure to deter at Dunkirk, 30
Lydd, 20

MacNaughton, Major General, 4
Maginot Line, 24, 34, 48
Malaspina, 166
Manella, Tetassi, 156
Manxman, 17
Maridian, 168–169
Marie Jose, 163
Maringliano, Francesco, 112
Massilia, 58, 59
Matilda tanks, 150
Menzies, Robert, 120
Metaxas, Ioannis, 155; death of, 161
Meuse Line, 109
MI5, 108–109, 111–112, 115–116, 117

MI6, 115
Milch, Erhart, 94
Miller, Joan, 112
Mona's Queen, 6–7, 10; attack on, 6; sinking of, 21
Monnet, Georges, 78
Montgomery, Bernard, 29, 38
Montrose, 19, 20
Morocco, 43
Musashi, 120
Mussolini, Benito, 43, 67, 68, 69, 134–135, 139, 143–144, 146, 150; decision to attack Greece, 141; declaring war on France and Britain, 43; Hitler's meeting with, 56–57, 141

Nautilus, 20
Neptunian, 168
Nicholson, Brigadier, 5
XIX Panzer Corps (Germany), 1, 8
Ninth Army (Germany), 88, 101
North Africa, 43, 55, 56, 75, 103, 120, 136, 142, 155, 161, 202
Norway, 17, 37

O'Connor, Richard N., 154–156, 157–158, 160
Oehrn, Victor, 162–164
Operation Catapult, 72–76
Operation Compass, 151
Operation Dynamo, 6
Operation Felix, 153
Operation Isabella, 153
Operation Sea Lion, 81–106, 127, 135, 152
Oriole, 21

Ostmark, 184
Owens, Arthur George, 115–116; as double agent, 116; imprisonment of, 116; report on British radar, 118; as triple agent, 116–117

Panzer Group Guderian (Germany), 40
Papagos, General, 152
Paris, 17
Paris: French government fleeing from, 47; German troops marching into, 46
Parona, Admiral, 186, 190
Passidon, 168
Pétain, Philippe, 36–39, 40–41, 44–45, 49–53, 55–57, 58, 60–61, 65, 68–70, 72, 77–80, 133, 139–141, 197, 198–200; appointment as prime minister, 50–51; conspiracy to unseat Reynaud, 49; decision to seek armistice with Germany, 51; as dictator, 78–80; opinion of De Gaulle, 40
Platon, Rear Admiral, 23
Poland, 130–133; partitioning of, 132
Pound, Dudley, 55, 149
Prague, 17, 31–32
Prien, Guenther, 109, 167–169, 171, 178, 192
Provence, 76

Raeder, Erich, 17, 63, 64, 65, 73, 83–91, 103–106, 107, 126, 130, 135, 137–139, 141–142, 153, 181, 185, 197
RAF: *See* Royal Air Force (Britain).

Ramsay, Archibald H. M., 112, 113

Ramsay, Bertram, 7, 13, 26–29, 30, 33, 36, 110

Reichstadt, Duke of, 201

Resolution, 137, 148

Reynaud, Paul, 24, 35–36, 40, 44–45, 49–51, 59, 77; agreement with Churchill on declaration of union between France and Britain, 50; asking U.S. for help, 49–50; Bullitt, meeting with, 39; collapse of Reynaud government, 51; meeting with Churchill, 5–6; Pétain's conspiracy to unseat, 49

Reysen, Hans, 117

Ribbentrop, Joachim von, 140

Richelieu, 137

Ripert, Minister, 201

Rommel, Erwin, 53, 155, 161

Roosevelt, Franklin D., 39, 49–50, 54, 112, 130–131, 179–181

Rougier, Louis, 198–202

Royal Air Force (Britain), 5–6, 13, 20, 30–31, 37–38, 40, 67, 83, 85, 89, 91, 92, 94, 95, 97–98, 101, 102, 103, 105, 107, 114, 121, 122, 154, 172–173, 184, 194; air raid on Berlin, 124–125; failure to deter Luftwaffe at Dunkirk, 30

Royal Navy (Britain), 6, 46, 85, 91, 97–98, 100–101, 115, 166

Royal Warwickshire regiment (Britain), 20

Rumania, 138, 141, 155

Rundstedt, Karl Rudolf Gerd von, 1–2, 39, 42, 88, 100

St. Abbs, 31

Salman, Otto, 191

San Giorgio, 148

Saxton-Steer, William, 109

Scarborough, 167–168

Scharnhorst, 73, 96

Scheer, 182

Schmid, Josef, 94

Schmidt, Minister, 64

Schmidt, Wyulf, 117

Scotia, 32

Second Panzer Division (Germany), 8

Sestini, Commander, 186

Seventh Armored Division (Britain), 153, 154, 156–159

Seventh Army (France), 41

Seventh Hussars (Britain), 144

Seventh Panzer Division (Germany), 41, 46

Seyss-Inquart, Arthur, 132

Sheaf Mead, 163

Sherbrooke, 168

Sherwood Foresters (Britain), 29

Shirer, William L., 65, 77, 85, 124–125, 141

Siegfried Line, 24

Singapore, 120, 145

Sixteenth Army (Germany), 88, 101

Sixth Army (Germany), 88

Sixth Division (Australia), 154

Sixtieth Division (France), 18

Snabb, 164

Somaliland, 143, 146

Somerville, James, 13, 73, 74, 76, 77

South Africa, 143

Spain, 139–140
Spanish Civil War, 31
Speer, Albert, 84
Spinel, 7
Spitfire fighter planes, 30
Strasbourg, 73, 76
Stuka dive-bombers, 31, 94, 95, 102
Sudan, 135, 147
Supreme Allied War Council, 44–45
Surcouf, 74

Tasso, 193
Telena, 163
Tellera, General, 160
Tennant, W. G., 11, 16, 21, 26, 27, 35
Tenth Army (France), 42, 61
Third Division (Britain), 38
XXXIX Army Corps (Germany), 46
Times (London), 198
Tippelskirch, Kurt von, 62
Titan, 167
Tobruk, 155–156
Trevisa, 174
Tripitz, 96
Twelfth Army (Germany), 42
Twentieth Motorized Division (Germany), 9
Twenty-second Italian Corps, 156

U-47, 109, 167
U-48, 171, 173, 174, 178
U-boats, 162–195
United States, 49, 54, 75, 86, 89, 130–131, 138, 165, 173, 180–181, 195, 197; freezing French assets in, 54; Lend-Lease program, 180–181; Reynaud asking help from, 49–50
Uruguay, 163
USS *Tuscaloosa*, 180

Valiant, 148, 150
Vanquisher, 193
Versailles Treaty (1919): *See* World War I.
Vichy government, 133, 198, 201, 203
Ville de Mons, 167
Viscount, 193

Wakeful, 19–20
Wake-Walker, W. F., 27–28, 30
Wavell, General, 135, 145, 146, 148, 149, 153, 154, 155, 159, 160–161
Weygand, Maxime, 40–45, 48–49, 51–53, 55–57, 60, 62–63, 64–66, 68, 78, 134, 202; demanding France ask Germans for armistice, 49; opinion of De Gaulle, 40
Whitshed, 34
Williams, Gwilym, 116
Wilson, Maitland, 150
Wolkoff, Anna, 112–113
World War I, 63, 77, 84, 108; armistice, 60, 62; Versailles Treaty, 60, 62, 63
Wrestler, 188

Yamato, 120